ANGELO TOSATO

THE CATHOLIC STATUTE OF BIBLICAL INTERPRETATION

A cura di Monica Lugato

G&BP
Pontificia Università Gregoriana
Pontificio Istituto Biblico
2021

Cover: Yattagraf srls - Tivoli (RM)
Impaginazione: Scuola Tipografica S. Pio X - Roma

© 2021 Pontifical Biblical Institute
Gregorian & Biblical Press
Piazza della Pilotta 4, 00187 - Roma
www.gbpress.org - books@biblicum.com

ISBN 978-88-7653-**734**-9

CONTENTS

EDITOR'S NOTE

This work, authored by Angelo Tosato in 1999, was translated from the original Italian version, *Lo statuto cattolico dell'interpretazione della Bibbia*, published in *Ars interpretandi. Annuario di ermeneutica giuridica,* vol. 4 (1999), *Interpretazione del sacro e interpretazione giuridica*, Padova, CEDAM, 1999, pp. 123-200 (re-published in ANGELO TOSATO, *Vangelo e ricchezza. Nuove prospettive esegetiche,* a cura di Dario Antiseri, Francesco D'Agostino, Angelo Petroni, Soveria Mannelli, Rubbettino, 2002)[1]. The hope is to more effectively reach the English speaking community thereby significantly expanding the access to this foundational contribution to the scientific debate on the interpretation of the Bible. I know that by undertaking this complex task, I not only fulfil one of my longstanding projects, but also one of my mother's, Maria Livia Tosato (Angelo Tosato's sister), greatest wishes.

We are very grateful to Prof. Jean Louis Ska, S.J., for having written the Foreword to this book: there could hardly have been a more apt person.

We are also grateful to Dr. Morgan Eleanor Harris for her substantial contribution to finalising the translation revision; and to Dr. Francesco Bianchi, who has helped with the footnotes, importantly on the Hebrew, Greek and Latin citations, and has drafted the various indexes.

To the publisher, Gregorian & Biblical Press, we are indebted for having made this publication possible; to the Rector of the Pontifical Biblical Institute, P. R. Michael Francis Kolarcik S.J., for accepting the volume in the "Fuori collana" Series and for His comments on a first version; to Mr. Basilio Mussolin and Mrs. Giovanna Ilaria for the promptness with which they have handled the editing process.

A few clarifications are in order. The references to "this century" in the translated text must be read as referring to the 20th century (as the original article was written and published in 1999). A note to that effect has been

---

[1] A previously published English translation of the article (in *Ars interpretandi. Journal of Legal Hermeneutics*, vol. 4/1999, *Interpretation of the sacred – Interpretation of the Law*, Padova, CEDAM, 2000, pp. 129-206), was regretfully inaccurate and published only after the Author's death, without him having the possibility to revise or approve the text.

added where needed in square brackets, accompanied by '*ed.*', for 'editor's note'.

Scripture passages quoted in English in this work are our translations of the same texts as found in the original version of the study: the original text of the article does not provide any indication as to which, if any, translation of the Bible the Author may have used.

Finally, we have translated the word "attualizzazione" with the term "actualization", even though the literal meaning of the English term can be understood differently. According to the Author, "attualizzazione" indicates the sapiential development of the original sense of the biblical text (which is known through exegesis) into a sense for the present times, what he calls an *actualized* sense (see section 2.1 (d) *infra,* and footnote 93 specifically). In deciding to translate this term as "actualization", we have found inspiration in the publication of the Pontifical Biblical Commission, *The Inspiration and Truth of Sacred Scripture. The Word that Comes from God and Speaks of God for the Salvation of the World* (transl. by T. Esposito, revised by F. O'Fearghail, Liturgical Press, Collegeville, 2014, p. 58): «Finally, the latest writings present an actualization of the ancient texts; the book of Sirach, for example, identifies the Torah with Wisdom».

The responsibility for any inaccuracies or mistakes remains exclusively mine. Such errors are plausible, considering on the one hand that the article is a highly scientific *summa* of the Author's lifelong study of the Bible and, on the other, that I lack any scientific competence on biblical exegesis and hermeneia. The Author's autobiography, and a list of his publications are also included in the Appendix to this volume.

Monica Lugato

FOREWORD

"There are no facts, only interpretations" – (Friedrich Nietzsche, *Notebooks*, Summer 1886 – Fall 1887). This famous sentence is certainly not to be found in Angelo Tosato's rigorous and exhaustive study on the official Catholic doctrine in the realm of Biblical interpretation. It is not present in its background either. The quote, however, may serve as a kind of master key to open all the latches of what may look, at first sight, as an unconquerable stronghold defended by heavily equipped garrisons of quotations in Latin, Greek, and Hebrew, and fortified by walls of Church documents. In what sense may we use Friedrich Nietzsche to cross the drawbridge and the several enclosures of Angelo Tosato's citadel? Simply because Friedrich Nietzsche's basic problem is, eventually, not much different from that treated in depth by Angelo Tosato in his essay. This is what I mean to say in these few lines of introduction.

Angelo Tosato (Venice, 1938 – Rome, 1999) is first of all a serious lawyer, with a profound knowledge of juridical questions and problems. His biblical dissertation on marriage in the Bible is a clear witness of his expertise in the field. The main problem treated in these pages is juridical as well. It has little to do with the relationship between facts and interpretation, however, but with the relationship between sacred texts, in this case, our Holy Scriptures, and their different classes of interpreters instead. These interpreters and their interpretations are all historically, socially, and culturally situated in particular contexts. The biblical texts, in all their variety, are also historically, socially, and culturally located and contextualized. In this sense, Angelo Tosato develops a line of thought which is close to the basic meaning of Nietzsche's sentence. In a few words, every affirmation depends on a certain perspective, the writer's perspective, and the interpreter's perspective. Angelo Tosato's question, however, is more specific. He treats the juridical problem raised by the interpretation of biblical texts within the Church and the Catholic Church in particular. This is the reason why he refers very often to official statements by councils and Church authorities.

With this bunch of keys in our hands, let us cross the drawbridge, namely the definition of the Bible for the Catholic faith, its nature and origin, its purpose and function, and its addressees. The Bible's origin and nature is both divine and human. Its purpose is the salvation of our world and of humankind, and its function is, among others, to provide the Church with a kind of rule of thumb in all its spheres of activities. Its addressees are all members of humankind and, in a special way, the faithful members of the Christian Church.

We can now enter the gate of a solid wall and discover the arsenals of an accurate biblical interpretation, its prerequisites, its criteria, and its forms. Among the prerequisites of a Catholic interpretation, let us notice the presence of a necessary affinity of the interpreter with the biblical text. Let us notice as well the necessity of an intelligent "elaboration of an actualised sense" alongside the exercise of exegesis. The latter endeavours to recover the original meaning of the text in its context and for its first audience. The former, called *hermeneia*, aims at translating the original meaning into the languages and cultures of the contemporary world.

As for the criteria, taking as example and model Jesus of Nazareth's controversies with his adversaries, Angelo Tosato furbishes his weapons, namely faithfulness to the literal sense of the Scriptures over against certain exegetical traditions, faithfulness to the intention of the text and faithfulness to the intention of the author.

The forms of Catholic interpretation depend, obviously, on the various categories of addressees. Angelo Tosato distinguishes with care five storehouses with five different kinds of guardians, namely all members of the human race, especially the people of good will; the faithful Christians; the Christian biblical scholars; the Christian theologians; the bishops, i.e., the members of the Church's Magisterium. Everyone is endowed with a special armour, i.e., with capacities, rights, and duties. One detail may draw the reader's attention. Angelo Tosato asserts, with solid reasons, that the juridical authority of the Magisterium is limited to the actualized interpretation of biblical texts for our world, and has not to deal with the proper exegetical and scientific task of recovering the original meaning of these texts. The Magisterium's decisions, moreover, can be modified, corrected, and rectified, as is the case with every human decision.

There is much more to discover and admire in this fortress. I just hope to have aroused the reader's curiosity and interest in visiting this castle with all its enclosures, towers, bastions, and batteries. Moreover, I hope that the reader may enjoy, after reaching a dungeon and looking through its crenels or an arrow hole, the vast and gorgeous panoramas of a truthful interpretation of our Scriptures.

For those who would like to extend and deepen their knowledge in this field, I can recommend a recent publication by the Pontifical Biblical Commission, *The Inspiration and Truth of Sacred Scripture: The Word That Comes from God and Speaks of God for the Salvation of the World*. Translated by Thomas Esposito and Stephen Gregg, reviewed by Fearghus O'Fearghail; foreword by Gerhard Ludwig Müller (Collegeville, MN: Liturgical Press, 2014). I can also advise to read an older essay on a similar topic, written during Vatican II, but still very relevant, Norbert Lohfink, *The Christian Meaning of the Old Testament*. Translated by R. A. Wilson (Milwaukee, MO: Bruce, 1968; London: Burns & Oates, 1969). Angelo Tosato's essay was written not long after another publication by the Pontifical Biblical Commission, *The Interpretation of the Bible in the Church* (1993). See, for instance, Joseph A. Fitzmyer, *The Biblical Commission's Document "The Interpretation of the Bible in the Church": Text and Commentary* (Rome: Pontifical Biblical Institute, 1995). Here is his position toward this document (cf. his footnote 3): "My aims are different from those of the document of the Pontifical Commission, of which I have made extensive use. However, the interested reader would do well to make its direct acquaintance. I do not claim that his interests cannot find greater satisfaction in that document than in this essay."

Let me wish to all perseverant and qualified readers, in a final word, a fruitful and enjoyable visit to Angelo Tosato's interpretative castle.

Jean Louis Ska

ANGELO TOSATO

THE CATHOLIC STATUTE
OF BIBLICAL INTERPRETATION

My concern here is not with interpretation in general but with biblical interpretation; not the interpretation which is carried out discretionally by individual readers according to the abilities, competences and interests, but rather that which is duly carried out by the members of the Catholic Church, in conformity with the rules of interpretation in force therein. Of this specific interpretation, I do not intend to examine the practice (what it is), but rather its statute (what it ought to be); and not in order to propose a personal theory on the matter, but rather to expound the official Catholic doctrine[1] as it has been and is being perfected in the field through over two thousand years of history, and above all in this last century [the XXth century, *ed.*][2]. The knowledge, understanding and formulation of this doctrine will obviously be my own. Mine too are certain insights and additions, as well as the indication and discussion of a few open issues. Finally, in the choice of topics and their arrangement, I have sought to take account of their possible comparative relevance in relation to the statute of the interpretation of the law in force within a constitutional state[3].

---

[1] I mean: the teaching of the Catholic hierarchy. The relevant documentation has been collected (incompletely) and translated (approximatively) in the *Enchiridion Biblicum. Documenti della Chiesa sulla Sacra Scrittura*, ed. A. Filippi and E. Losa, 2nd ed., Bologna: EDB, 1994. For the readers' greater convenience, I shall indicate it in the citations with the acronym *EB*. For the texts of Vatican II – except for those included in *EB* – I shall make use of *Documenti. Il Concilio Vaticano II*, Bologna: Ed. Dehoniane, 1966 [= *C.Vat.II - Doc.*].

[2] This process of refinement is not the product of abstract speculation, whether philosophical (within the general theory of interpretation), or theological (within the general theory of biblical interpretation). Rather, it has been the practical problems raised in the course of history (especially modern history) by its interpretative practice which have prompted the advances and doctrinal adjustments. Likewise, the statement regarding the Son applies also to the Church: didicit ex iis quae passus est obœdientiam (Heb 5,8). [All references to "this last century" are to the XXth century, the article having been written and published in 1999, *ed.*].

[3] It need not be cause for surprise if my presentation will turn out to be very different from that of a recent and in many ways praiseworthy document of the PONTIFICAL BIBLICAL COMMISSION, *L'interprétation de la Bible dans l'Église* [= *IntB*], Città del Vaticano: Libreria Editrice Vaticana, 1993; dated 15 April 1993, but published on 18 November 1993, headed by the important Discourse *De tout cœur* [= *Dtc*] of JOHN PAUL II (23 April 1993) and a "Preface" by the Commission's President, the [then, *ed.*] Prefect of the Congregation for the Doctrine of the Faith, Card. J. Ratzinger (the three texts are reproduced in *EB* 1239-1258; 1259-1263; 1264-1560). My aims differ from those of the document of the Pontifical Commission, of which I have made extensive use. However, the interested reader would do well to make direct acquaintance with it. His interests may find greater satisfaction in that document than in this essay.

1. *The Bible*

The Catholic statute of biblical interpretation is fundamentally determined by the Catholic faith in the Bible.[4] It seems as if an unwritten principle is at work here, one which can be formulated in the following terms: *quidquid recipitur ad interpretandum, non ad modum recipientis, sed ad modum recepti interpretandum est.*[5] To clarify the elements of this statute, it is therefore necessary to begin by recalling the truths of this faith. The exposition that follows will be limited to those truths which appear to be most essential. They concern: (1) the origin and the nature of the Bible; (2) its purpose and its functions; and (3) its destinations[6].

1.1 *Origin and nature of the Bible*

Concerning the *origin* and thus the *nature* of the Bible, there are two complementary and inseparable truths of faith: (a) its true divinity; (b) its true humanity.

(a) *The true divinity of the Bible.* The first and fundamental truth affirms that all the books of the Bible – of the Old and of the New Testament, with all their parts, such as they have been received by the Church – since they are inspired by God, have God as their "Author"[7]. They are, therefore,

---

[4] For the followers of Jesus Christ, the Bible is an object of faith (cf. Jn 2,22: οἱ μαθηταὶ αὐτοῦ ... ἐπίστευσαν τῇ γραφῇ καὶ τῷ λόγῳ ὃν εἶπεν ὁ Ἰησοῦς cf. 5,47). See more extensively below, in 1.1 and in 1.2. About the birth of this faith, see ORIGEN, *De principiis*, IV, 1, 6 (PG 11, 115; GCS 5, 301-302).

[5] I have given the principle the form of a Latin adage, shaping it on and contrasting it with the well-known adage *quidquid recipitur ad modum recipientis recipitur*, to which a great a part of contemporary "hermeneutics" seems to be very devoted. But it can be proposed in a simpler form: *As the object to be interpreted, so the proper mode of its interpretation.* The principle applies – as we shall see – to the Catholic interpretation of the Bible. It also applied, in my opinion, to the ancient juridical interpretation by the Romans, at least judging from the axiom which they handed down to us, almost *regula regularum*: "Non ex regula ius sumatur, sed ex iure quod est regula fiat" (D. 50.17.1). I believe that this holds true for every interpretation intended to be faithful (cf. below, in 2.1, a).

[6] In the Document *Interpretationis problema* [= *Ip*] (31 October 1989), B, I, 2 (*EB* 1206), on the interpretation of dogmas, the INTERNATIONAL THEOLOGICAL COMMISSION writes: "Ex ipsa nuntii biblici essentia modus resultat interpretationis". In fact, a clearer understanding of the nature of the Bible has led the Catholic Church to an adjustment of its interpretive statute.

[7] VATICAN II, Dogmatic Constitution *Dei Verbum* [= *DV*] (18 November 1965), § 11 (*EB* 686): "[Libri integri tam Veteris quam Novi Testamenti, cum omnibus eorum partibus]

"divine Scriptures", "Sacred Scriptures"[8], "Word of God"[9]. The Bible has a divine nature.

The official Catholic magisterium has reaffirmed this truth on several occasions in this last century [the XXth century, *ed.*], although it has always been explicitly present in the faith of the universal Church. It initially did

---

Spiritu Sancto conscripti (cf. Jn 20,31; 2Tim 3,16; 2 Pet 1,19-21; 3,15-16), Deum habent auctorem"; similarly at § 16 (*EB* 694). Cf. Council of Trent, *Decretum primum de Sacris Scripturis* [= *DSS-I*] (8 April 1546; *EB* 57); Vatican I, Dogmatic Constitution *Dei Filius* [= *DF*] (24 April 1870), chap. II (*EB* 77).

As the numerous biblical citations of *DV* § 11 suggest, this article of faith is already present in the primitive Church. 2Tim 3,16 states: πᾶσα γραφὴ θεόπνευστος. Significant, too, are the recurring expressions in the NT, γέγραπται (in absolute form, with *passivum divinum*, e.g. Mt 4,4), γέγραπται διὰ τοῦ προφήτου (e.g. Mt 2,5), γεγραμμένον (e.g. Jn 6,31). In 1Thess 2,13, Paul is pleased that the word brought by him has been received for what it is, the divine Word. The writings of the OT attest that this faith was already present in Israel. For example, one reads that the tables of the Law are: *ketuvîm bᵉ'eṣba' 'elohîm*, "written with the finger of God" (Ex 31,18); *ma'aśeh 'elohîm hemmah, wehammiktav miktav 'elohîm hû', ḥarût 'al-halluḥôt*, "they are the work of God, and the writing it is the writing of God, carved on the tables" (Ex 32,16); this is repeated in Ex 24,12; 34,1; Deut 4,13; 5,22; 9,10; 10,2.4 (in Ex 34,27-28, instead, it is Moses who puts them in writing upon the divine order). Neh 8 speaks without distinction of the "book of the Law of Moses that YHWH had given to Israel" (v. 1), the "book of the Law of God" (v. 8), and the book of the "Law given by YHWH through Moses" (v. 14); in 2Chr 34,14, of the "book of the Law of YHWH".

[8] This is the language typically used in magisterial documents. Already in Rom 1,2, one finds ἐν γραφαῖς ἁγίαις, and in 2Tim 3,15 ἱερὰ γράμματα. The adjective only states explicitly a qualification that is implicit, yet manifest, in the way that the NT speaks emphatically of these books as ἡ γραφή, αἱ γραφαί: they are "the Scripture", "the Scriptures". The later, now common, denomination "the Bible" (τὰ βιβλία "the Books") bears the same semantic value.

[9] Vatican II, *DV*, § 9 (*EB* 682): "Sacra Scriptura est locutio Dei quatenus divino afflante Spiritu scripto consignatur"; "consignatur" should probably be corrected into "consignata est", as suggested by the sense and the following § 10: "Divinitus revelata, quae in Sacra Scriptura litteris continentur et prostant, Spiritu Sancto afflante consignata sunt"); "Sacrae ... Scripturae verbum Dei continent et, quia inspiratae, vere verbum Dei sunt", *DV* § 24 (*EB* 704); cf. §§ 10.12.13.14.17.21 (*EB* 683.688.691. 692.695.701). This is traditional doctrine. See, for example, Gregory the Great, *Epistola ad Theodorum* (June 595; *EB* 31); Council of Trent, *Decretum secundum de sacris Scripturis* [= *DSS-II*] (8 April 1546; *EB* 64). It is also the living doctrine: at the end of the liturgical reading of biblical passages, the faithful acclaim: "Word of God!", "Word of the Lord!".

The NT has as equivalents of γέγραπται (mentioned above), the expressions ἐρρέθη (e.g. Mt 5,21), θεὸς εἶπεν (e.g. Mt 15,4), τὸ ῥηθὲν ὑπὸ κυρίου διὰ τοῦ προφήτου (e.g. Mt 1,22), followed by citations of scriptural passages. There are similar expressions in the OT; e.g. Jeremiah's letter to the exiles, which exhorts: "Thus says the Lord of hosts, the God of Israel..." (Jer 29,4).

so, at the time of modernism, to rebut the theory that scriptural inspiration
was limited to the spheres of faith and moral teachings[10]; then, in the days
of Nazi anti-Semitism, to condemn those who expunged from the Bible,
as non sacred, the books of the Old Testament[11]; finally, at the time and
in the documents of the Second Vatican Council, to recall the ministerial
character of its mission, to establish the principle of its reform and to lay
the premises for fruitful ecumenical dialogue[12].

(b) *The true humanity of the Bible.* The second truth perfects the first,
affirming that these same books, although inspired by God, also have as
their authors, their "true authors", their respective human writers (the
so-called "hagiographers")[13]; they are therefore divine Scriptures in truly
human writings. Word of God in truly human words[14]. In brief, the faith
recognizes in the Bible the reality of a divine "co-descendance", the pres-

---

[10] Leo XIII, Encyclical Letter, *Providentissimus Deus* [= *PrD*] (18 November 1893),
EB 124-125; Congr. S. Rom. Et Univ. Inquisitionis, Decree *Lamentabili* [= *Lam.*]
(4 July 1907), § 11 (*EB* 202); Pius X, Encyclical Letter, *Pascendi dominici gregis* [= *Pasc.*],
(8 September 1907), *EB* 263.

[11] Pius XI, Encyclical Letter. *Mit brennender Sorge* (13 March 1937; *Acta Apostolicae
Sedis* 29, 1937, 150-151): "The sacred books of the Old Testament are exclusively the Word
of God and constitute a substantial part of his Revelation...". Cf. M. Gilbert, in P. Laghi,
M. Gilbert and A. Vanhoye, *Chiesa e Sacra Scrittura. Un secolo di magistero ecclesia-
stico e studi biblici* (Subsidia biblica, 17), Roma: Ed. Pont. Bibl. Inst., 1994, pp. 26-27.

[12] Vatican II, *DV*, §§ 12. 13. 14. 17. 24. 26 (*EB* 688. 691. 692. 695. 704. 708); cf.
Decree on Ecumenism *Unitatis redintegratio* [= *UR*] (21 November 1964), §§ 3 and 21
(*EB* 504 and 561-564). The conciliar constitution *Dei Verbum* is to be understood against
the background of the ecumenical enthusiasm that animated the sessions of the synodal
assembly right from its first announcement (cf. *Acta et Documenta*, Series I, vol. I, Città del
Vaticano: Typis Polyglottae Vaticanae, 1960, p. 6).

[13] "In sacris vero libris conficendis Deus homines elegit, quos facultatibus ac viribus
suis utentes adhibuit, ut Ipso in illis et per illos agente, ea omnia eaque sola, quae Ipse
vellet, ut veri auctores scripto traderent", Vatican II, *DV* § 11 (*EB* 686). Already in the
Encyclical Letter *Divino afflante Spiritu* [= *DaS*] (30 September 1943; *EB* 556), Pius XII
had written: the human author "in sacro conficiendo libro est Spiritus Sancti ὄργανον seu
instrumentum, idque vivum ac ratione praeditum,... divina motione actum, ita suis uti[*tur*]
facultatibus et viribus, 'ut proprium uniuscuiusque indolem et veluti singulares notas ac
lineamenta' ex libro, eius opera orto, facile possint omnes colligere". The quotation is taken
from Benedict XV, Encyclical Letter *Spiritus Paraclitus* [= *SpP*] (15 September 1920),
EB 448.

[14] Vatican II, *DV* § 12 (*EB* 688): "Cum... Deus in sacra Scriptura per homines more
hominum locutus sit...".

ence of a mystery of "incarnation"[15]. Analogously to Jesus Christ, the Bible
has both a truly divine and truly human nature; it has a "theandric" nature[16].

The official Catholic magisterium came to affirm this truth only about fifty
or so years ago [mid Ninties, *ed.*], after centuries of labour. It designates both
the surrender to an evident truth and the solution to the difficulties raised by the
thousands of imperfections in the biblical books[17].

1.2 *Purpose and function of the Bible*

As for the *purpose* of the Bible, the Church believes that the sacred
books are ordered, ultimately, to the salvation of human beings[18]. This is
their one and only concern.

---

[15] VATICAN II, *DV* § 13 (*EB* 691); PIUS XII, *DaS* (*EB* 559); JOHN PAUL II, *Dtc* §§ 4; 6-15
(*EB* 1242; 1245-1257).

[16] We can further develop, I think, the analogy between Jesus Christ and the Bible and
say: as Jesus Christ was in all ways like human beings, except for sin, so too the sacred
Scripture is in all ways like human books except for sin.

[17] The turning point came with PIUS XII, *DaS* (*EB* 556). It was reached through the
adoption of a new conception of scriptural inspiration (cf. *EB* 556 and 559). Traditionally,
the scriptural inspiration was thought of as a kind of divine "dictation" (cf. COUNCIL of
TRENT, *DSS-I, EB* 57: "Spiritu Sancto dictante... a Spiritu Sancto dictatas..."), so that the
true humanity of the sacred Scriptures was compromised. Yet their true divinity was also
compromised, given the innumerable imperfections of the sacred books.

[18] VATICAN II, *DV* § 11 (*EB* 687): the books of Scripture teach the truth "quam Deus nostrae salutis causa Litteris Sacris consignari voluit"; cf. also *DV* § 7 (*EB* 677); *DV* § 10 (*EB*
685). The COUNCIL OF TRENT, *DSS-I* (*EB* 57), had spoken of "salutaris veritas" (VATICAN
I, *DF*, *Prooemium* (in H. DENZINGER and A. SCHÖNMETZER, *Enchiridion Symbolorum*, ed.
36 amended, Herder, Barcinone etc. 1976 [= *DS*], n° 3000), of "salutaris doctrina", but in
reference to its *own* doctrine). Cf. Rom 1,16: the Gospel, on which, according to Christians,
converge all the writings both of the Old and New Testaments, "is the strength of God for
the salvation of each believer". See also Jn 20,30-31; 1 Jn 1,2.
　　Incidentally the Council text speaks of "salvation" (*salus*), and not, as is usual for the
Church (even the CIC of 1983 does so, can. 1752), of the "salvation of souls" (*salus animarum*). This expression, in contrast with the former, is not appropriate. Indeed, it reflects
the erroneous idea that the final goal of the Christian "salvific economy" would be the
spiritual, heavenly and individual well-being of people when, according to the Revelation
of the OT and the NT, it is the integral well-being of humanity (spiritual *and material*,
heavenly *and earthly*, individual *and social*; human beings are not solely spiritual, nor
solely heavenly nor solely individual creatures). It is perhaps helpful to recall THOMAS:
"gratia non tollit naturam, sed perficit et supplet defectum naturae" (*Summa theologiae*, I,
q.1, 8 ad 2; q.2, 2 ad 1; II-II, q.188, 8c).

The official magisterium was pushed to reaffirm, still in this last century [the XXth century, *ed.*], this tenant of faith – however elementary – due to the obstinate insistence of some (who had clearly not learned from the case of Galileo) to judge the validity of the discoveries of the human sciences according to their concordance, or lack thereof, with the biblical writings[19].

With regard to the *functions* of the Bible, the Church believes that, in the pursuit of the said aim, the sacred books have a threefold instrumental function[20]: the first, formal, documentary in character, in relation to the divine Revelation; the second, substantial, kerygmatic-didactic in character, in relation to humankind; the third, also substantial, normative in character (on belief and conduct), in relation to the Church.

The first function, formal and documentary in character, can be indicated by qualifying the biblical books (together with the apostolic tradition) as a "source (of knowledge) of the Revelation"[21], and precisely in the sense

---

[19] LEO XIII, *PrD* (*EB* 121); PIUS XII, *DaS* (*EB* 539). Both documents find support in a passage of AUGUSTINE, *De Genesi ad litteram*, 2, 9, 20 (PL 34, 270s; CSEL 28, sectio 3, pars 2, p. 46), where one reads that the sacred writers and their divine Inspirer did not intend to instruct human beings on matters (such as, for example, the inner fabric of visible things) "nulli saluti profutura".

[20] In truth, the documents of the official magisterium sometimes speak of the Bible in such a way as to suggest it is bestowed with a directly salvific function. The written divine Word in fact is said to be: "bread of life" (VATICAN II, *DV*, § 21; *EB* 701), "power of God for the salvation of anybody who believes" (VATICAN II, *DV*, §§ 17 and 21; *EB* 695 and 701; cf. § 11; *EB* 687; cf. Rom 1,16), "pure and everlasting source of the spiritual life" (VATICAN II, *DV*, § 21; *EB* 701; cf. § 26; *EB* 708). Clearly, however, the language here used is metaphorical. Its final effect is enhanced by images, but the means by which this is achieved is not determined. These means (upon which we shall dwell shortly) are, substantially, those of making known (*kérygma*), teaching (*didaché*) and prescribing (*entolé*), provided though that they are then joined by faith and works; cf. 2Tim 3,15: "Ever since your infancy you have known the holy Writings, that can instruct you for salvation through the faith that is in Christ Jesus".

[21] Cf. LEO XIII, *PrD* (*EB* 114): the divine books hold an eminent place "inter revelationis fontes"; PIUS XII, Encyclical Letter *Humani generis* (12 August 1950; *EB* 611) which speaks of "divinae Revelationis fontes", of "sacrae fontes", in reference to the "Sacred Writings" and to the "divine Tradition". It is true that VATICAN II preferred to avoid this formulation (it appeared in the very title of the preparatory scheme: *De fontibus Revelationis*). It was in fact employed by some to propose the Tradition as a parallel source, autonomous from and in competition with the Bible. This misunderstanding can be avoided – it seems –, by referring to "source" in the singular.

Apparently similar, albeit different in content, is the expression used by the COUNCIL OF TRENT, *DSS-I* (*EB* 57) and taken up by VATICAN II, *DV* § 7 (*EB* 677), with reference to the Gospel: "*fons* omnis et salutaris veritatis et morum disciplinae". The Gospel is discussed

that they are written testimony, a certifying documentation of Revelation[22], carried out by God through words and deeds within human history[23], and culminating in Jesus Christ (his person, his proclamation, his teaching, his death and resurrection, and the gift of his Spirit to his followers)[24].

This teaching brings to light the correct relationship between sacred Scripture and divine Revelation. These two entities must not to be seen as one and the same; the former is not to be taken for the latter. Scripture supports and is functional to Revelation, it certifies its existence and content (its occurrence in history and the teachings which have been drawn from it; from which the kerygmatic, didactic and preceptive functions of Scripture derive). It does so by providing certainty in the knowledge of Revelation, yet knowledge that always corresponds to the degree of understanding achieved by the human authors upon inspiration. In Scripture, therefore,

---

here (as Revelation, indirectly also as Scripture) and is spoken of as a "*fons*" to emphasize its "canonical" function in relation to the doctrine of faith and of morals of the Church (cf. *infra*, the third function). The true, final, inexhaustible "source" (in the sense of "canon") of the Christian doctrine is Revelation, not Scripture (the latter is so in a derived and subordinate way). Scripture is rather the "source" of Revelation (in the sense that it provides knowledge of it, is authentic witness to it).

[22] VATICAN II, *DV* § 7 (*EB* 677), links the writing down of the "objects" revealed ("quae Deus… revelaverat") with their perpetual and integral transmission ("ut in aevum integra permanerent omnibusque generationibus trasmitterentur"); *DV* § 17 (*EB* 695): "Quarum rerum [the events of Christian Revelation] scripta Novi Testamenti extant testimonium perenne atque divinum". In an equivalent way, *DV* § 14 (*EB* 692) speaks of the writings of the Old Testament in relation to the "economy of salvation" established by God with the people of Israel. Cf. Ex 32,15; Rom 3,21; Jn 19,35; 21,24; 1 Jn 1,1-4.

Less appropriately, in my view, Scripture (and Tradition) are spoken of as means of "transmission" of the Revelation (cf. VATICAN II, *DV* §§ 1 e 7, *EB* 669 e 677). Rather, it is the Church (after Israel), in its concrete historical existence and as mystery-sacrament of salvation, that should be regarded and indicated as the Organ of transmission of Revelation (cf. *LG* § 9). As such, the Church is likewise attested by the Scripture in a documentary way.

[23] VATICAN II, *DV* §§ 2 and 4 (*EB* 670 and 672); cf. INTERNATIONAL THEOLOGICAL COMMISSION, *Ip*, B, I, 1 (*EB* 1203): "Revelatio, quam sacra Scriptura testificatur, verbis et gestis in Dei historia cum hominibus locum habet".

[24] VATICAN II, *DV* §§ 2, 4 and 7 (*EB* 670, 672 and 677); INTERNATIONAL THEOLOGICAL COMMISSION, *Ip*, B, I, 1 (*EB* 1203).

we find only a dim reflection of Revelation[25], which remains, in its intrinsic divine transcendence, an inexhaustible mystery to the human mind[26].

The second function, substantial and kerygmatic-didactic in character, is determined by the fact that the Christian Revelation, of which the sacred books are written testimony, bears a communicative content, which is first and foremost the proclamation (*kérygma*) and instruction (*didaché*) of universal salvation: it is "Gospel"[27].

This teaching does not seem to have been thematically developed to date, but it was lived with particular intensity in the sessions of the last Council [Vatican II, *ed.*][28].

---

[25] Metaphorically and with a daring hyperbole, *DV* § 7 (*EB* 678) writes that Tradition and Scripture "veluti speculum sunt, in quo Ecclesia in terris peregrinans contemplatur Deum". Paul makes a different use of this metaphor in 2Cor 3,18; 4,6. Even more distinctive is its use by James in Jas 1,23.

[26] Cf. VATICAN I, Dogmatic Constitution *Dei Filius* (24 April 1870) [= *DF*], chap. II (*De revelatione*) (*DS* 3005); VATICAN II, *DV* §§ 5 and 6 (*EB* 674 and 675); INTERNATIONAL THEOLOGICAL COMMISSION, *Ip*, B, I, 1 (*EB* 1205).

It is necessary to pay attention not to misunderstand the sense in which the conciliar documents speak of Revelation as "contained" (e.g. VATICAN I, *DF*, chap. II, *EB* 77: "continetur") in the sacred books (and in the divine Tradition). More accurately, it is some *elements of knowledge* deriving from Revelation that are "contained", "contained and expounded" (cf. COUNCIL OF TRENT, *DSS-I*, *EB* 57: "contineri"; VATICAN II, *DV* § 11, *EB* 686: "continentur et prostant").

[27] The whole of Revelation, recorded by the sacred Scriptures (OT and NT), on account of its communicative content (that of promise, proclamation, and explanation of the divine "economy" of salvation) is not inappropriately designated as "Gospel" (*euaggélion*). Cf. COUNCIL OF TRENT, *DSS-I* (*EB* 57): "quod [Evangelium], promissum 'ante per prophetas in scripturis sanctis' (Rom 1,3; cf. Jer 31,22s; Is 53,1; 55,5; 61,1 *et alia* Heb 1,1f), Dominus noster Iesus Christus, Dei Filius, proprio ore primum promulgavit, deinde per suos apostolos... omni creaturae praedicari iussit (cf. Mt 28,19ff; Mk 16,15ff.)"; VATICAN II, *DV* §§ 14-17 (*EB* 692-695). This "Gospel" is not to be separated from "Teaching" (*didaché, didaskalía*). Cf. COUNCIL OF TRENT, *DSS-I* (*EB* 57): the apostles have the task of preaching the Gospel "tamquam fontem omnis et salutaris veritatis et morum disciplinae"; VATICAN II, *DV* § 11 (*EB* 687): "Scripturae libri veritatem, quam Deus nostrae salutis causa Litteris Sacris consignari voluit, firmiter, fideliter er sine errore docere profitendi sunt". The conciliar text continues by citing 2Tim 3,16-17: "all Scripture... is useful for teaching (ὠφέλιμος πρὸς διδασκαλίαν)...". See also: Rom 15,4: εἰς τὴν ἡμετέραν διδασκαλίαν; 1Cor 10,11: πρὸς νουθεσίαν ἡμῶν.

[28] This is amply attested in the documents of VATICAN II. See, for example, Dogmatic Constitution *Lumen gentium* [= *LG*] (21 November 1964), § 1 (*C.Vat.II - Doc.*, 284); *DV*, *Proœmium* (*EB* 669); Pastoral Constitution *Gaudium et spes* [= *GS*] (7 December 1965), §§ 1 and 3 (*C.Vat.II - Doc.*, 1319 e 1322-1323); the inaugural discourse of [ST.] JOHN XXIII

The third function, substantial and normative in character, arises from the fact that the Christian Revelation, of which the sacred books are written testimony, bears within itself a communicative content that is also and inseparably norm (*entolé*) of belief and conduct for the acquisition of salvation; that is, moreover, salvific "Covenant"[29] (*berît*), and salvific to such a pervasive extent, as to succeed in bestowing the sacred books with the title of Old and New "Testament", that is, Old and New "Covenant"[30].

Having regard to this normative function, the biblical books are traditionally described as "canonical"[31]. This adjective serves to indicate less the fact that these books belong to the "canon" (to the officially defined list of the biblical books), but instead their normative function (as "canon", "rule") for the Church. At least, this is how the formula has been explained. In fact, it is professed, for example: "[Ecclesia] eas [divinas Scripturas] una cum sacra Traditione semper ut supremam fidei suae regulam habuit et habet... omnis ergo praedicatio ecclesiastica sicut ipsa religio christiana sacra Scriptura... regatur oportet".[32]

---

and the messages transmitted by the synodal Fathers at the opening and closing of the Council (*C.Vat.II - Doc.*, pp. 968-980; 990-1006).

[29] The "œconomia christiana" is described by VATICAN II, *DV* § 4 (*EB* 673) as "fœdus novum et definitivum". The sacred books perform a preceptive-normative function for all those who, having welcomed the Christian proclamation of salvation, have freely adhered to the New Covenant. This "normative" function is more specific compared to the "didactic" one, although it comprises an essential component of the latter; cf. Mt 28,19-20: "make disciples of all nations, baptising..., teaching them to observe all that I have prescribed to you", μαθητεύσατε πάντα τὰ ἔθνη, βαπτίζοντες... διδάσκοντες αὐτοὺς τηρεῖν πάντα ὅσα ἐνετειλάμην ὑμῖν. The biblical teaching first of all gives the proclamation of the salvation offered in Christ Jesus, then teaches how this should be made one's own through obedience to Christ in faith and works, by adhesion to his Covenant.

[30] As is well known, the term "testament" is to be traced back (through the Latin *testamentum* and the Greek διαθήκη) to the Hebrew term *berît*, whose proper meaning is that of "covenant"/"treaty" (the current translation, "alliance", is not exegetically correct). Which specific human model of "covenant"/"treaty" the sacred authors had in mind when they conceived and described as a *berît* the legal bond between God and his people has yet to be fully clarified. The prevailing theory identifies the model with the international covenants stipulated between imperial sovereigns and subject sovereigns; however, it also seems possible to identify the model with the national (constitutional) covenants stipulated between a monarch (or one claiming to be a monarch) and the "elders", chiefs of clans and chiefs of tribes; compare Deut 33,3-5 with 2Sam 5,1-3; 2Kgs 11,17b and 2Chr 23,3.

[31] COUNCIL OF TRENT, *DSS-I* (*EB* 60); VATICAN I, *DF*, chap. II and related can. 4 (*EB* 77 and 79); VATICAN II, *DV* § 11 (*EB* 686).

[32] VATICAN II, *DV* § 21 (*EB* 701). Cf. *LG* § 15 (*C.Vat.II - Doc.*, 325): sacred Scripture as *norma credendi et vivendi*; and *DV* § 7 (EB 677): "[Christus Dominus] mandatum

With these solemn and binding pronouncements, the hierarchical mag-isterium seems to seek to resolve the doubts, that have historically arisen from its practice and continue to do so at times today, regarding its faith in the absolute primacy of the Word of God in the Church or, at least, regarding its intentions to truly respect the supreme authority of this Word.

Given the decisive impact of this article of faith, it could be beneficial to ponder on the foundation of the normativity of the Scripture for the Church, to enucleate in detail its all-encompassing scope and to reaffirm its functional character in relation to the salvific aim.

As for the *foundation*, it is necessary to make clear that: *(a)* the pri-mordial nucleus of the sacred Scriptures are the two tables of stone (*luḥot 'even, luḥot 'avanîm*)[33] on which God inscribed the ten "words" (the *devarîm*), the commandments of the Decalogue[34]; *(b)* these "words" are accompanied, as their detailed specification, by a body of "norms" (the *mišpatîm*), "decrees" (the *ḥuqqîm*) and "laws" (the *tôrôt*), which God transmitted orally to Moses with the order to put them in writing[35]; *(c)* the corpus of the *devarîm*, extended by the *mišpatîm*, *ḥuqqîm* and *tôrôt*, con-stitutes the "document (book) of the Law" (the *sefer hattôrah*)[36]; *(d)* this legislative body represents the "document (book) of the Covenant" (the

---

dedit Apostolis ut Evangelium… tamquam fontem omnis et salutaris veritatis et morum disciplinae omnibus praedicarent" (cf. above, fn. 21). This last phrase follows a passage of Council of Trent, *DSS-I* (*EB* 57). The conclusion of the *DSS-I* also should be cited. Having listed *nominatim* all and each of the "sacred and canonical books" of the Bible one by one, and having pronounced the anathema on those who refuse to accept them as such, the Conciliar Fathers write: "Omnes itaque intelligant, quo ordine et via ipsa synodus, post iactum fidei confessionis fundamentum, sit progressura, et quibus potissimum testimoniis ac praesidiis in confirmandis dogmatibus et instaurandis in ecclesia moribus sit usura" (*EB* 60).

[33] Ex 24,12; 31,18; 34,1; Deut 4,13; 5,22(19); 9,10.

[34] Ex 24,12; 34,1.28; Deut 4,13; 5,22(19); 9,10; 10,2.4. Cf. Ex 20,1 and Deut 5,22(19).

[35] Ex 21,1 (introductory verse to the body of the *mišpatîm*, which extends until Ex 23,19 and which is commonly called the "Covenant Code", on the basis of the expression *sefer habberît*, "document of the covenant", of Ex 24,7); Ex 24,3; Deut 27,3; 31,24.

[36] Deut 28,61; 29,19.20; 30,10; 31,26; Josh 1,8; 8,31.34; 23,6; 24,26; 2Kgs 14,6; 22,8.11; 2Chr 17,9; 34,14.15; Neh 8,1.3.8.18; 9,3.

sefer habberît)[37], the text containing the clauses of the treaty[38], that Israel stipulated with YHWH, its God; *(e)* this pact-based normative is not only moral law (rule for the consciences), nor only religious law (rule of the relations between human beings and God, regulation of worship), but also truly juridical law (rule of the relations between fellow citizens and of citizens with foreigners); it is, better still, true legislative order (constitutional charter, civil code, criminal code and code of criminal procedure), which gives rise to and firmly establishes Israel as the people of YHWH and as the holy nation[39]; *(f)* the Jewish sacred Scriptures are, therefore, ultimately *tôrah*, "Law", and more precisely, *berît*, "(Law of the) Covenant"; (g) the new holy Scriptures of Christian origin, which adopt and integrate the old ones[40], are fundamentally testimony to the new Covenant and the new Law, that Jesus Christ established and enacted to renew and perfect the ancient Covenant and the ancient Law[41], and that represent the foundational event and the constitutive order of the Church, as the new people of God and as

---

[37] Ex 24,7; 2Kgs 23,2.21; 2Chr 34,30. The same *devarîm*, the ten "words", are called *divrê habberît*, "words of the covenant" (Ex 34,28) because "on the basis of these words I have sanctioned the covenant with you and with Israel" (Ex 34,27; cf. Ex 24,8); elsewhere, the *devarîm* themselves are designated in abbreviation as *berît*, "covenant", Deut 4,13.23; cf. Sir 45,5; the tables with the *devarîm* are called *luḥot habberît*, "tables of the covenant" (Deut 9,9.11.15; Heb 9,4).

[38] It is to the "provisions" of the covenant that one ought probably refer the word *'edût/'edut*, usually translated as "testimony", that is found used in the expressions *luḥot ha'edut*, "the tables of the testimony" (Ex 31,18; 32,15; 34,29), that is, "tables of the provisions of the covenant", and *'arôn ha'edut*, "the ark of the testimony" (Ex 25,22; 26,33; 40,21; Deut 10,8), that is, the wooden chest where the two "tables of the covenant" are kept (Ex 25,16; Deut 10,2.4; 1Kgs 8,9 // 2Chr 5,10). Sometimes the word *'edut* also is used alone (Ex 25,16.21; 40,20) to indicate, through synecdoche, the "words of the covenant", the "tables of the covenant".

[39] Cf. Ex 19,3-8 and 24,1-11; cf. Deut 29,9-14; Josh 24,1-27; 2Kgs 23,1-3; Ezra 7; Neh 8. Acceptance of the Law is the condition for the acquisition of "citizenship", of membership in Israel; as far as many norms are concerned, observance of the Law is condition for retaining "citizenship" (for example, with reference to some matrimonial norms: Ezra 9-10; this will also in part apply for membership in the Church, new Israel: Acts 15; 1Cor 5).

[40] Cf. VATICAN II, *DV* § 16 (*EB* 694).

[41] Mt 26,28; Lk 22,20; 1Cor 11,25; Heb 7,22; 8,6-13; 9,15; 12,24. It is worthwhile to recall the messianic texts of the Old Testament's prophecy: "I, YHWH,... have shaped you and have made you as Covenant of the people (*le-berît 'am*), as Light of the nations (*le-'ôr gôjim*)" (Is 42,6; cf. 49,8); "Behold my Servant whom I uphold,... he will bring law to the nations (*mišpat laggôjim jôsî'*),...he will bring law according to truth (*le'emet jôsî' mišpat*)" (Is 42,1.3).

the new holy nation[42]. Accordingly, the Bible is not only a tale, a narrative (kerygmatic and didactic) text, but also and principally a law, a legislative text; and the narrative part is functional to the legislative one, not *vice versa*[43].

As for the comprehensive *scope* of the normativity of the Bible, it can be useful (even if somewhat pedantic) to list in full. Therefore: *(a)* The normativity of Scripture extends over each and every one of the members of the ecclesial community (including those who hold governance positions within it), as also over the entire "Church" community [44]. *(b)* This normativity of the Scriptures in the ecclesial domain encompasses the entire life of the Church: its practices, but even before that, its doctrine[45]; and not only the teachings of its scholars and their magisterium, but also that of the members of its hierarchy and their magisterium[46]. *(c)* This normativity of the Scriptures in the doctrinal-ecclesial sphere extends both over the doc-

---

[42] 1Pet 2,9-10; Rom 9,25-26; 10,19; Rev 21,3. Cf. VATICAN II, *LG* §§ 6 and 9 (*C.Vat.II - Doc.*, 295 and 308); *UR* § 2 (*C.Vat.II - Doc.*, 498); JOHN PAUL II, *Catechism of the Catholic Church* [= *CCC*] (11-10-1992), §§ 871 and 1267-1268.

[43] It is the need for certainty about the normative content of the law (*a fortiori*, therefore, of divine Law) that leads to the desire for a *written* law. See what was written as early as in the epilogue to the Hammurabi's Code.

[44] As for the individual faithful, suffice it to remember that they do not become members of the "people of God" unless they adhere to the Covenant (cf. above, fn. 39); they do not enter into the "family" of Jesus Christ, unless they obey the will of God (Mt 12,46-50). Consider also the formula of the Tridentine anathema (*DSS-I*; *EB* 60): "Si quis autem libros ipsos [those named in the above written list] integros... pro sacris et canonicis non susceperit...: anathema sit". As for the rulers, there is no need to recall that within the community of Jesus Christ, by the explicit command of the "Founder", all are "brothers", and the "first" must become "last", "servants" to the others (cf. Mt 20,24-28; 23,8.11-12; Jn 13,1-17). The OT orders the king to submit to the Law (Deut 17,18-20; cf. Josh 1,7-8). After all, one of the foremost reasons that has always given rise to the desire for *written and public* laws is precisely to subtract the law from being manipulated by those that hold power and to likewise place them, as far as possible, *sub lege*. As for the Church in its generality, see the texts in fn. 32.

[45] Cf. the texts in fn. 32. The statement "omnis ergo praedicatio ecclesiastica sicut ipsa religio christiana sacra Scriptura... regatur oportet" (on which, see above) is somewhat ambiguous, but it seems to seek to indicate both sectors of the Church's life, that of doctrine and that of practice. Should it be understood as referring solely to practice, the magisterial specifications in the following notes apply to doctrine in any case.

[46] VATICAN II, *DV* § 10 (*EB* 684): "Quod quidem Magisterium [the *vivum Ecclesiae Magisterium*; to be understood as the hierarchical magisterium of pope and bishops in communion with him] non supra Verbum Dei est, sed eidem ministrat, docens nonnisi quod traditum est". Obviously, the same provision is valid for the scholarly magisterium as well.

trine on the truths to be believed (dogmatic theology) and the doctrine on the precepts to be put in practice (moral theology)[47]. *(d)* This normativity of Scripture in the realm of moral theology extends both to the doctrine on ethical action (ethical theology, commonly identified with "moral theology"), as well as to the doctrine on juridical action (theology of law)[48]. *(e)* This normativity of the Scriptures in the sphere of the theology of law extends both to the scholars of the doctrine and to their magisterium, but even before that, to the Church's legislators and codifiers, to their legislations and codifications, to their laws and their codes[49]. *(f)* This normativity of the Scriptures in the realm of the Church's legal order extends not only to matters codified by the Church, but also to matters that have not been codified, those that should have been included in the *Lex fundamentalis,*

---

[47] VATICAN II, in *DV* § 24 (*EB* 704) affirms: "sacra theologia in verbo Dei scripto, una cum sacra Traditione, tamquam in perenni fundamento innitur... sacrae Paginae studium sit veluti anima sacrae theologiae"; and in the Decree *Optatam totius* [= *OT*] (28 October 1965), § 16 (*EB* 661): "sacrae Scripturae studio, quae universae theologiae veluti anima esse debet, peculiari diligentia alumni instituantur... Theologia dogmatica ita disponatur, ut ipsa themata biblica primum proponantur... Item ceterae theologicae disciplinae ex vividiore cum Mysterio Christi et historia salutis contactu instaurentur". This is followed by an explicit reference to moral theology (that has to be perfected, *perficienda*, with special care; which must be nourished with scriptural doctrine to a greater extent) and to canon law: "similiter in iure canonico exponendo... respiciatur ad Mysterium Ecclesiae...".

These Conciliar directives reverse the traditional structure of theological work: no longer is sacred Scripture the *ancilla* of theology (dogmatic and moral; that is: Scripture is no longer to be used *a posteriori* to confirm a pre-made ecclesiastical, hierarchical doctrine), but theology is the *ancilla* of sacred Scripture. The older (reprehensible and officially condemned) approach is found, for example, in COUNCIL OF TRENT, *DSS-I* (*EB* 60; noted above, in fn. 32: "in confirmandis dogmatibus"); LEO XIII, *PrD* (*EB* 114: "theologo minime negligenda est ipsa demonstratio dogmatum ex Bibliorum auctoritate ducta").

[48] The conclusion stems from the magisterial passages cited in the previous footnote. In addition to the sole specific reference to canon law (in *OT* § 16, *EB* 661), one must recall the insistence on subsuming the *whole* of theology *(universa theologia, theologia dogmatica... item ceterae theologicae disciplinae, universa theologiae disciplina)* to Scripture (*ibidem*).

[49] In the Apostolic Constitution promulgating the new *Codex Iuris Canonici* (*Sacrae disciplinae leges*, 25 January 1983), JOHN PAUL II, writes: "Altera oritur quaestio, quidnam sit Codex Iuris Canonici. Cui interrogationi ut rite respondeatur, mente repetenda est longinqua illa hereditas iuris, quae in libris Veteris et Novi Testamenti continetur, ex qua tota traditio iuridica et legifera Ecclesiae, tamquam a suo primo fonte, originem ducit". And shortly thereafter: "Codex, utpote cum sit primarium documentum legiferum Ecclesiae, innixum in hereditate iuridica et legifera Revelationis et Traditionis, pernecessarium strumentum est...". See also *Decretum Gratiani*, I Pars, Distinctio 9, can. 11.

planned (not accomplished) as a Constitutional Charter to be set as basis and rule of the *Codex Iuris Canonici*[50].

As for the *functional character* of the Bible's normativity, it must be always borne in mind that this normativity, just like that of every legislative code, is not an end in itself, but rather ordered to the good of each and every member of the community in which it is in force as a legal order[51]. In the specific case of the Bible, it is ordered to the salvific purpose, already mentioned above.

1.3 *The destinations of the Bible*

As for the *destinations* of the Bible, the Church believes that God has destined his Scriptures not only to certain people, but to all; and that he has provided not for a single type of destination, but rather for different and complementary types, which can be distinguished on the basis of the identity of the receivers and of the title under which the Bible is destined to them.

Therefore, it is useful, first of all, to distinguish between a *universal, beneficial* destination and an *ecclesial, ministerial* destination of the Bible. The first type of destination (a) is that aimed at all human beings as members of humanity[52]. The Bible is destined to them for their personal benefit. They are constituted as *receivers* (*simple receivers*, pure beneficiaries) of

---

[50] This can be inferred from the fact, explained above, that for Christians the Bible is not only *sefer hattôrah*, but also *sefer habberît*.

[51] Behold – Moses proclaims –, I have set before you today [with the Book of the Law] life and good (*'et-haḥajjîm we'et-haṭṭôv*),.." (Deut 30,15; cf. Deut 32,47: the words of the Law are *ḥajjêkem*, "your life"; Sir 45,5: *tôrat ḥajjîm*", "law of life"); "observe His laws and His commandments for your good (*'ašer jîṭav*) and the good of your sons after you" (Deut 4,40; cf. Deut 5,29.33; 6,24 and *passim*). "If you want to enter into life – Jesus reminded a man –, observe the commandments" (Mt 19,17). Cf. Thomas, *Summa Theologiae*, I-II, q. 99, a. 1, in corpore: "manifestum est quod de ratione praecepti est quod importet ordinem ad finem, inquantum scilicet illud praecipitur quod est necessarium vel expediens ad finem".

[52] The universal destination of the Gospel – the Gospel promised by God through the Prophets, fulfilled and enacted by Jesus Christ, witnessed to and preached upon his command by the Church – concerns primarily its living transmission (that of the community of believers with the works and the words of their lives), cf. Mt 28,19-20; Acts 1,8; but, secondarily, and as a necessary consequence, its written communication also (the one of the sacred books, that have their center of convergence in the Gospel and that of the Gospel constitute the authentic documentation), cf. Vatican II, *DV* §§ 1. 7. 17 (*EB* 669. 677-678. 695).

the biblical Word. The second type of destination (b) is that aimed at all Christians as members of the Church. The Bible is destined to them not just for their personal benefit (as it is for all human beings), but also as an onus, with the task of performing a service for the benefit of others. Besides being receivers, these are constituted also as servants (*receivers-ministers*, onus-bound beneficiaries) of the biblical Word.

It is furthermore useful to distinguish (with reference to this ministerial-ecclesial destination) between a type of *common* destination and other various and complementary types of *specific* destination. The common destination is that aimed at all believers in Christ, as parties to the New Covenant and members of the Church. The Bible is assigned to them for deposit in safekeeping and for their testimony. These are constituted, not just, generically, as receivers-ministers, but also, specifically, as *depositaries-holders* of and *witnesses* to the biblical Word[53]. The specific destinations, on the other hand, are those aimed at individual categories of Christians, to each for its specific additional ministry.

Among the latter, it is best to distinguish: (c) a destination for the divulgation, and this specifically concerns the vast and varied category of the preachers and catechists; these, as well as beneficiaries, depositaries and witnesses, are also constituted in the ministry of *disseminators* of the bibli-

---

[53] "Depositaries". VATICAN II, *DV* § 10 (*EB* 684) writes: "sacra Traditio et sacra Scriptura unum verbum Dei sacrum depositum constituunt Ecclesiae commissum, cui inhaerens tota plebs sancta pastoribus suis adunata in doctrina Apostolorum ... iugiter perseverat (cf. Act 2,42), ita ut in tradita fide tenenda, exercenda profitendaque singularis fiat antistitum et fidelium conspiratio". This important passage was introduced in the conciliar text starting with the Scheme of September 1964, accompanied by the following illustration: "Hac periodo, ex integro nova, statuitur relatio unius depositi revelati, quod Traditione et Scriptura constituitur [...], ad totam Ecclesiam, quae *simplices fideles simul ac hierarchiam* [italics of the original text] complectitur. Hoc autem fidei depositum intelligendum est Ecclesiae esse commissum, non ut authentice illud interpretetur (quod ad solum magisterium spectat), sed ut ipsa de eodem vivat, ac ita vivendo Ecclesia cuiusque aetatis Ecclesiam apostolicam fideliter imitetur"; cf. F. GIL HELLÍN, *Concilii Vaticani II Synopsis. Dei Verbum, Città del Vaticano*: LEV, 1993, p. 74. See also JOHN PAUL II, *CCC* §§ 84 and 857 (cf. also the *incipit* of the Apostolic Constitution *Fidei depositum*, issued for the publication of the *Catechism*).

"Witnesses". VATICAN II, *LG* § 35 (*C.Vat.II - Doc.*, 374) writes, for example: "Christus... suum munus propheticum adimplet non solum per hierarchiam, quae nomine et potestate Eius docet, sed etiam per laicos, quos ideo et testes constituit et sensu fidei et gratia verbi instruit (cf. Acts 2,17-18; Rev 19,10), ut virtus Evangelii in vita quotidiana, familiari et sociali eluceat". Cf. *LG* § 10 (*C.Vat.II - Doc.*, 311); and cf. JOHN PAUL II, *CCC* §§ 904-905.

cal Word[54]; (d) a destination for the scientific research of the original sense, and it specifically concerns the category of biblical scholars; these, as well as beneficiaries, depositaries and witnesses, are also constituted in the ministry of *interpreters-exegetes* of the biblical Word[55]; (e) a destination for the prudential elaboration of its meaning for the present day ['attualizzazione', in the original, *ed.*] and this specifically concerns the category of theologians; these, as well as beneficiaries, depositaries and witnesses, are also constituted in the ministry of *interpreters-hermeneuts* of the biblical Word[56]; (f) a destination for the issuing of the judgment on the correctness of the interpretation (hermeneutics), and this specifically concerns the category of bishops[57]; these, as well as beneficiaries, depositaries and witnesses, are also constituted in the ministry of *interpreters-judges* of biblical interpretation (of *hermeneia*)[58].

The exclusivity of the bishops' prerogative to issue judgement on the interpretation (hermeneutics) of the Bible is traditional practice and doctrine[59]. The warning to theologians that "sacrae Paginae studium sit veluti

---

[54] VATICAN II speaks of those, whom I have designated as "disseminators", as "divini verbi administri", whose task it is "plebi Dei Scripturarum pabulum fructuose suppeditare" (*DV* § 23; *EB* 703); and it speaks of their *munus* as of a "ministerium verbi, pastoralis nempe praedicatio, catechesis omnisque instructio christiana", that "verbo Scripturae… salubriter nutritur sancteque virescit" (*DV* § 24; *EB* 704). Thus, the conciliar document uses – less appropriately, in my view – a generic qualification ("ministers of the divine word"), applicable not only to the specific category under examination, but also equally well to other specific categories (those designated here by the letters b, d, e, f).

[55] Cf. VATICAN II, *DV* § 12 (*EB* 688-690); § 23 (*EB* 703).

[56] Cf. VATICAN II, *DV* §§ 23 and 24 (*EB* 703 e 704). This distinction between *interpreters-exegetes* and *interpreters-hermeneuts* anticipates the conceptual and terminological clarifications which will be developed *infra*, in 2.1. Take it for now as a provisional classification.

[57] The passage of *DV* § 10 (*EB* 684), cited in fn. 53, goes on to say: "Munus autem authentice interpretandi verbum Dei soli vivo Ecclesiae magisterio concreditum est, cuius auctoritas in nomine Iesu Christi exercetur". See, as explanation, the words with which the *Rapporteur* presented the opening sentences of § 10 to the Council Fathers (cf. above, fn. 53). See also JOHN PAUL II, *CCC*, § 85.

On the way this *"authentice interpretandi"* of *DV* §10 ought to be understood, as well as on this limitation to the scope of the episcopal jurisdiction to issue judgement on the correctness of biblical interpretation (it seems to be restricted to *hermeneutic* interpretation), we shall return *infra*, in due place (in 2.3).

[58] The reservation in fn. 56 above applies to *"hermeneia"* as well.

[59] As for practice, it suffices to here simply recall the role played by the ecclesiastical government in defining the canon of the sacred Books, in controlling their publication and explanation, and in setting the norms for their interpretation. As for doctrine, see: COUN-

anima sacrae Theologiae", has been issued in this last century [the XXth century, *ed.*] with increasing insistence[60]. Since Pius XII, encouragement to biblical scholars to persevere in their studies and praise of their task (*munus adeo excelsum*) have found expression[61]. The call to the preachers and to the catechists not to separate the performance of their ministry from the study of the Scriptures resounds powerfully in the last Council [Vat. II, *ed.*][62]. Recognizing the faithful as "depositaries" (not just "recipients") of the sacred Scriptures, with a consequent reconsideration of the specific office of the bishops, occurred only in the course of the last Council [Vatican Council II, *ed.*][63], within the context of a general rethinking of the proper relationship between the people and the governing authorities in

---

CIL OF TRENT, *Decretum secundum de Sacris Scripturis* [= *DSS-II*] (*EB* 62): "... sancta mater Ecclesia, cuius est iudicare de vero sensu et interpretatione scripturarum sanctarum"; PIUS IV, *Professio fidei tridentina* (13 November 1564; *EB* 73); VATICAN I, *DF,* chap. II (*EB* 78); LEO XIII, *PrD* (*EB* 108-109); Apostolic Letter *Vigilantiae* [= *Vig.*], (30 October 1902) (*EB* 142); VATICAN II, *UR* § 21 (*EB* 660).

In order to correctly understand these passages, one must bear in mind that the term "Ecclesia" is used here, inappropriately, to indicate the governing *authority* of the Church, the *official magisterium* of the hierarchy, and not the *community as a whole* of believers. This use – symptomatic of a conception of the Church in which the hierarchy, so to speak, "subsumes" the community – was so deeply rooted that it even resurfaced in the documents of Vatican II, and even in the *DV* itself (at § 12) in relation to the matter under examination. The text reads: "Cuncta enim haec, de ratione interpretandi Scripturam, *Ecclesiae iudicio* ultime subsunt, quae verbi Dei servandi et interpretandi divino fungitur mandato et ministerio" (the emphasis is mine). Taken literally ("Ecclesia" = community of believers in Christ), the statement would be antithetical to that of *DV* § 10 (reported in fn. 57). But the *intentio auctorum* is different. In presenting the third scheme of *DV* (that of 1964, which introduced this version of the phrase), the *rapporteurs* explained that they had added "quaedam verba [the dependent clause "quae verbi Dei..."] *de munere hierarchici magisterii* ". Cf. GIL HELLÍN (cit. in fn. 53), p. 102.

[60] LEO XIII, *PrD* (*EB* 114); BENEDICT XV, *SpP* (*EB* 483); VATICAN II, *DV* § 24 (*EB* 704); OT § 16 (*EB* 661).

[61] PIUS XII, *DaS* (*EB* 569); VATICAN II, *DV* § 23 (*EB* 703); JOHN PAUL II, *Dtc* § 16 (*EB* 1258).

[62] VATICAN II, *DV* §§ 23, 24 and 25 (*EB* 703, 704 and 705).

[63] The second scheme of *DV*, that of 1963 (*De divina revelatione*), at § 9 bore the title "Utriusque [= Tradition and Scripture] relatio ad S. Magisterium", and stated: "s. Scriptura ac s. Traditio, uti sacrum verbi Dei depositum, non singulis hominibus, sed vivo et infallibili Ecclesiae Magisterio concreditum est". But already the third scheme, that of 1964, at § 10 (ex § 9-10) bore the title "Utriusque relatio *ad totam Ecclesiam et* Magisterium", and corrected the text to how it was to appear in the definitive draft (reported in fn. 53). Cf. GIL HELLÍN, cit. in fn. 53, pp. 74-76.

the Church[64]. While the universal destination of the sacred books is found in recent [writh respect to 1999, *ed.*] magisterial documents, it has not yet been made the subject of adequate reflection in the faith.[65]

2. *Biblical interpretation*

The truths of faith recalled above govern Catholic statute of the interpretation of the Bible. The exposition which follows does not claim to be exhaustive (far from it). Its sole purpose is to highlight some elements of this statute that are deemed to be important. We shall focus on: (1) the requirements of biblical interpretation; (2) its criteria; (3) its forms.

2.1 *The requirements of biblical interpretation*

Each and every interpretative activity is subject to a multitude of requirements: some generic, owing to the genus "interpretation"; others specific, owing to the type of interpretation and determined by the *quem* and by the *quid interpretandum* proper to each type. Certainly, the Catholic faith in the "theandricity" of the Bible leads the Church to distinguish this text from every other; but not to exempt its interpretation from being subject to requirements: neither to the generic requirements of interpretation, nor to those specific of the interpretation of texts, nor to those, even more specific, of the interpretation of ancient texts and of normative texts. On the contrary, such faith causes some of these requirements to assume particular scope and relevance. It is these which deserve our attention. We shall examine four of them, namely: (a) the requirement of faithfulness, that is, of a moral virtue; (b) the requirement of affinity, that is, of possessing spiritual endowments; (c) the requirement of exegesis, that is, of a

---

[64] The rethinking took concrete shape in the doctrine of Vatican II, *LG*, chapters II and III.

[65] John Paul II, *Dtc* § 15 (*EB* 1526): we are in the year 1993. Although they were animated by a profound sense of the Church's responsibility towards humanity as a whole – attested, among other things, by the Constitution *GS* and the messages addressed to the whole world at the opening and closing of the Council –, the Fathers of the Vatican Council II close the Constitution *DV* with a chapter entitled *De sacra Scriptura in vita Ecclesiae*. The CCC similarly concludes its exposition of the doctrine concerning Scripture (§§ 131-133). However, given that the Bible has a salvific purpose (cf. above, 1.2) and that God "desires that all human beings be saved and come to knowledge of the truth" (1Tim 2,4; cf. 4,10), there can be no doubt about the universal destination of the sacred books.

scientific enquiry of the original meaning (of the original meanings); (d) the requirement of *hermeneia*, that is, of a theological elaboration of an 'actualised' sense, that is, a meaning for the present times (of 'actualised senses', that is, of meanings for the present times).

(a) *The requirement of faithfulness.* Every human activity, to be *human*, must have as its foundational element, its basic condition, the requirement of morality. In interpersonal relationships morality takes the form of justice, *constans et perpetua voluntas ius suum cuique tribuere*[66]. As far as interpretive activity, *in toto genere suo*, is concerned, the virtue of justice takes the specific form of the virtue of faithfulness to the "what" and to the "whom" to be interpreted [67]. More particularly, for the interpretation of a text, the first requirement is faithfulness to the text and to its author. This requirement also applies, and to the highest degree, to the Catholic interpretation of the Bible. Indeed, faith in the true *divinity* of the Bible leads us to cultivate religious sentiments towards this Text and its Author, sentiments made of piety and veneration[68].

---

[66] JUSTINIAN, *Institutiones*, I.1.1; cf. I.1.3; ULPIAN, D.1.10.1. It is well known that, for Christians, morality in interpersonal relations is not limited to justice; it also includes charity. However, charity does not replace justice; it perfects it. The first exercise of charity towards the neighbour is *ius suum cuique tribuere*.

[67] To reduce the *quid* and the *quem interpretandum* to the interpreting subject is an immoral act.

[68] The COUNCIL OF TRENT, *DSS-I* (*EB* 56), begins with a solemn declaration: the conciliar fathers ("Sacrosancta... Synodus"), recognizing that it is the Gospel of the Lord that is found in the books of Scripture and in the unwritten apostolic traditions, "pari pietatis affectu ac reverentia suscipit et veneratur". LEO XIII, in *PrD* (*EB* 90), writes: "Prudentiae debetur diligentiaeque Ecclesiae cultus ille Scripturae sacrae per aetatem omnem vividus et plurimae ferax utilitatis". VATICAN II, *DV*, Proemio (*EB* 669), goes further: "Dei Verbum religiose audiens..., Sacrosancta Synodus..."; and then returns to the theme in § 21 (*EB* 701): "Divinas Scripturas sicut et ipsum Corpus dominicum semper venerata est Ecclesia..." (in truth, this statement is rather bold, at least if it is referred to historical practice, and very demanding; so much so that the PONT. COMM. DECRETIS CONCILII VATICANI II INTERPRETANDIS was quickly called to rule on it, and did so with a restrictive interpretation, cf. *EB* 710).

On the slopes of Sinai, the people of Israel receive the divine words while standing, at a due distance, and in a state of cultic purity (Ex 19,10-25). At the reading of the Book, those present rise to their feet (Neh 8,5). So, too, do the faithful today, at the proclamation of the Gospel.

As the "depositary" of the sacred Scriptures[69], the Church knows that it is bound, first and foremost, to fidelity to the biblical Word in its "materiality". It must have great care for the text, preserving the script in its integrity, keeping intact (and, where necessary, critically restoring) its content[70]. Indeed, the sacred Scriptures have a definitive and immutable[71], inviolable character[72]. They do not allow alterations ("you shall not add anything to them, and you shall not take anything away from them")[73]. Unfaithfulness to the text is profanation, sacrilege.

Hence the care of the Church's official magisterium to define and defend the canon (= the list) of the sacred books[74], to establish the "authentic" text

---

[69] Cf. above, point 1.3, b ("depositaries"). The Book constitutes (together with the apostolic Tradition) a s*acrum depositum*, VATICAN II, *DV* § 10 (*EB* 683). The term "deposit" appears already in the NT (παραθήκη, 1Tim 6,20; 2Tim 1,12.14) with reference to the apostolic traditions (*depositum fidei*, cf. INTERNATIONAL THEOLOGICAL COMMISSION, *Ip*, C II, 1; *EB* 1219). The use of a juridical notion is not by chance. The obligations of the depositary towards the depositor and related to the "deposit" (*piqqadôn*) were well known in Israel starting in antiquity; cf. Ex. 21,6-7.9-12; Lev 5,21-26.

Ancient Israel kept the tables of the Law inside the Ark, the equivalent of our tabernacle (Ex 25,16; Deut 10,2.5).

[70] VATICAN II, *LG* § 25 (*C.Vat.II - Doc.*, 346 and 347): the *depositum divinae Revelationis* is "sancte custodiendum"; "praelucente Spiritu veritatis in Ecclesia sancte servatur"; *DV* § 10 (*EB* 684): "illud [verbum Dei scriptum et traditum], ex divino mandato et Spiritu Sancto assistente,... sancte custodit". It is already so in the NT. It is necessary to "safekeep" (φύλαξέιν), cf. 1 Tim 6,20; 2 Tim 1,12.14; it is necessary to "preserve" (κρατεῖν, "hold firmly"), cf. Rev 2,25; 3,11.

[71] Cf. VATICAN II, *DV* § 21 (*EB* 701): "..., cum a Deo inspiratae et *semel pro semper* litteris consignatae, [divinae Scripturae] verbum ipsius Dei *immutabiliter* impertiant, atque in verbis Prophetarum Apostolorumque vocem Spiritus Sancti personare faciant" (my emphasis). This is already biblical doctrine: "In truth I tell you: until heaven and earth shall pass away, not one iota or sign shall pass from the Law [= the Torah, the sacred Book], until all be fulfilled" (Mt 5,18). *Verbum Dei manet in aeternum*: Is 40,8; 1Pet 1,25; cf. Mt 24,35 (// Mk 13,31; Lk 21,33). Also: Num 22,18; 24,13.

[72] Jn 10,35: οὐ δύναται λυθῆναι ἡ γραφή "Scripture cannot be 'undone' ", annulled. Cf. Jer 36.

[73] Deut 13,1: *lo'-tosef 'alajw welo' tigra' mimmennû*; cf. Deut 4,2; 5,22; Prov 30,6; Qoh 3,14; Rev 22,18-19.

[74] COUNCIL OF CARTHAGE (28 August 397; = *Breviarium Hipponense*, can. 47, in *Collectio Hispana*, ed. Ch. Munier, CCL 149, Turnhout 1974, p. 340; cf. *EB* 16-20); INNOCENT I, Letter *Consulenti tibi* (20 February 405; *EB* 21-22); COUNCIL OF FLORENCE, Bull *Cantate Domino* (4 February 1442; *EB* 47); COUNCIL OF TRENT, *DSS-I* (*EB* 58-59).

There was no initial clarity in the Church on the exact content of the canon, as still attest, for example, the COUNCIL OF LAODICEA (c. 360; *EB* 11-13) and the *Apostolic Consti-*

(that which is definitively authoritative)[75], and to promote research into its genuine dictates[76].

---

tutions (end of the IV cent.; P.-P. JOANNOU, *Discipline générale antique*, in *Fonti*, fasc. IX, t. I, 2, Grottaferrata 1963, pp. 51-52, can. 85).

[75] Only in the XX century, and after overcoming long and strenuous opposition, did the official Catholic magisterium come to have a mature doctrine in this field. The COUNCIL OF TRENT, *DSS-II* (*EB* 61), enquiring into which, among the many editions of the Bible in circulation, should be held to be authentic ("quaenam pro authentica habenda sit"), "statuit et declarat, ut haec ipsa vetus et vulgata editio, quae longo tot saeculorum usu in ecclesia probata est, in pubblicis lectionibus, disputationibus, pradicationibus et expositionibus pro authentica habeatur…". VATICAN I, *DF*, chap. II (*EB* 77) limited itself to reaffirming the Tridentine declaration. LEO XIII, *PrD* (*EB* 106), while asking, out of respect for the Tridentine provision, that the vulgate version be taken as the basis for teaching, adds: "Neque tamen non sua habenda erit ratio reliquiarum versionum quas christiana laudavit usurpavitque antiquitas, maxime codicum primigeniorum. Quamvis enim, ad summum rei quod spectat, ex dictionibus Vulgatae hebraea et graeca bene eluceat sententia, attamen si quid ambigue, si quid minus accurate inibi elatum sit, "inspectio praecedentis linguae", suasore Augustino (*De doctrina christiana*, III, 4; PL 34, 68), proficiet". In the same Encyclical (*EB* 97), a few pages before, the use of the original texts is praised: "Exquisitius homines nostri in nativo Bibliorum codice… elaborare coeperunt". PIUS XII, *DaS* (*EB* 547) takes a further, decisive step in establishing the superior authority of the original text over its versions. He writes: "Primigenium illum textum explanari oportet, qui ab ipso sacro auctore conscriptus maiorem auctoritatem maiusque pondus habet, quam quaelibet, utut optima, sive antiqua sive recentior conversio". A couple of years earlier, in a *Letter to the Bishops of Italy* by the PONTIFICAL BIBLICAL COMMISSION (20 August. 1941; *EB* 522-533), issued by order of Pius XII and following his approval, it was clarified that the Council of Trent had declared the Vulgate "authentic" "in a juridical sense" (for public use, at that time), "but it did not intend in any way to prejudice the authority of the ancient versions,… and still less the authority of the original texts"; this would be a claim "not only contrary to common sense, which will never accept that a version could be superior to the original text, but also contrary to the mind of the Fathers of the Council [of Trent], as it appears from the Acts" (*EB* 526-527). PIUS XII returned to this topic in *DaS* (*EB* 549): "eiusmodi *authentia* non primario nomine *critica*, sed *iuridica* potius vocatur". VATICAN II, *DV* § 22 (*EB* 702) limits itself to recommending that modern translations be made "praesertim ex primigeniis Sacrorum Librorum textibus".

[76] In its obscurantist battle against "modernism", the Catholic hierarchy found a way to rebuke textual criticism as well; cf. PIUS X, *Pasc.*, *EB* 263; IDEM, Motu proprio *Sacrorum Antistitum* (1 September 1910), *EB* 343 (one of the points of the anti-modernist oath formula). It is to the credit of LEO XIII (Apostolic Letter *Vigilantiae*, 30 October 1902; *EB* 142), and still more of PIUS XII (*DaS*; *EB* 547-548) that it was officially rehabilitated in the Catholic Church. Pius XII refers to AUGUSTINE, and, appropriately, cites one of his passages (from the *De doctrina christiana*, II, 21; PL 34, 46): "Codicibus emendandis primitus debet invigilare sollertia eorum qui Scripturas divinas nosse desiderant, ut emendatis non emendati cedant". JOHN PAUL II, *Dtc* § 7 (*EB* 1246) and again the PONTIFICAL BIBLICAL COMMISSION, *IntB*, I, A, 3 (*EB* 1281) returned to this subject.

As it is called to interiorize, to put into practice and to spread what God communicates through the Scriptures[77], the Church has always known that it is also bound, above all, to be faithful to the biblical Word in its communicative "substantiality"[78]. It must give the most careful attention to the semantic content of the text, dedicating its efforts to understanding, living and transmitting what the Author said (the "letter") and has intended to say in it (the "spirit"). Understanding requires, in the case of this text, a ceaseless effort. This is so because the Word to be understood is not simply the word of another, but (through faith) the Word of the Other. It transcends all complete understanding; it encloses, yet only faintly discloses, the unfathomable mystery of the divine

---

[77] As is to be expected within a culture where oral communication is prevalent, this call is expressed first and foremost with the exhortation to "listen": *šema' jiśra'el*, "hear, O Israel" (Deut 6,4; cf. Deut 4,1; 5,1; 33,7; Is 48,12; 51,1.7; 66,5). The attitude of believers is that of Samuel: *dabber jhwh kî šomea' 'avdekâ*, "speak, Lord, your servant is listening!" (1 Sam 3,9.10). "Listening" must be followed by learning (*ûlemadtem*, "and learn", Deut 5,1; cf. Deut 31,11-13; *wehajû haddevarîm ha'elleh... 'al-levaveka*, "these words be on your heart [= in your mind]", Deut 6,6; cfr. Prov 6,21; Is 51,7), observance (*šemor-leka*, "observe", Ex 34,11; cf. Deut 4,40; 12,28; Prov 4,4; 7,1.2), practice ('*aśah*, "do", Deut 5,1; cf. Deut 6,24; 11,22), and teaching (*hôdîa'*, "make known", Deut 4,9; cf. Ex 10,2; 13,8; Deut 6,7.20-25). It is necessary to behave according to what is written in the Book, Josh 1,8 (cf. 1 Cor 4,6: stand by what is written; however, the passage is obscure; on it see, most recently, R.L. TYLER, "First Corinthians 4:6 and Hellenistic Pedagogy", *The Catholic Biblical Quarterly* 60, 1998, 97-103). There must be no deviating neither to the right nor to the left, from the ways fixed by God, Josh 1,7 (cf. Deut 5,32-33; 17,20; 28,14; Is 9,14-15; 19,15). This is equally so for the NT, no less than for the OT. Jesus recognizes as his own mother and brothers "those who hear the word of God and put it into practice" (Lk 8,21; cf. Lk 11,28; Jn 8,55). He himself is anxious to fulfil his Father's will: μὴ τὸ θέλημά μου ἀλλὰ τὸ σὸν γινέσθω, "not my will but yours be done" (Lk 22,42); οὐ τί ἐγὼ θέλω ἀλλὰ τί σύ (Mk 14,36; cf. Jn 4,34; 5,30; 6,38; Heb 10,7.10); "thy will be done", Mt 6,10. James exhorts his readers to receive the word of God with meekness, to put it into practice and to remain faithful to it, *Jas* 1,21-25 (cf. *Rev* 1,3). It is necessary to discern the will of God, Rom 12,2 (cf. Phil 1,9-10; Col 1,9; Eph 5,10.17).

[78] The Apostle Paul writes: "Everyone regard us as ministers of Christ and stewards of the mysteries of God; now, what is required of stewards is that each be found faithful", Οὕτως ἡμᾶς λογιζέσθω ἄνθρωπος ὡς ὑπηρέτας Χριστοῦ καὶ οἰκονόμους μυστηρίων θεοῦ. ὧδε λοιπὸν ζητεῖται ἐν τοῖς οἰκονόμοις ἵνα πιστός τις εὑρεθῇ (1Cor 4,1-2). Cf. Jn 13,16: "A servant is not greater than his master, nor an apostle greater than the one who sent him"; Lk 12,42-44 (// Mt 24,45-51). The word of God is not to be falsified, 2Cor 4,2 (cf. 1Thess 2,4; 2Tim 2,15: σπούδασον σεαυτὸν δόκιμον παραστῆσαι τῷ θεῷ, ἐργάτην ἀνεπαίσχυντον, ὀρθοτομοῦντα τὸν λόγον τῆς ἀληθείας).

(το μυστηρίον τοῦ θεοῦ)[79]. The divinity of Scripture perpetually poses the need to seek its meaning.

Hence the commitment of the recent official magisterium of the Church to promote the study of the sacred books[80] and to reiterate the objective to which the interpretative work of its scholars must be directed. Working in the service of the Church and in favour of humanity as a whole, interpreters must devote themselves to determining the literal meaning, in order to grasp the genuine meaning, that is, the mind of the Author, what the Author intended to say with his words. "Non quid ipse [interpres] velit, sed quid sentiat ille, quem intepretatur"[81].

(b) *The requirement of affinity.* In order to make a faithful interpretation, it is not sufficient that the interpreter has the virtue of faithfulness. It is not enough to *want* to be faithful, it is also necessary *to be able* to be so. In particular, in order to interpret a text, one has to have the capacity to understand it; and this comprises, in addition to those intellectual, cognitive and sapiential faculties appropriate to the text (with which we shall deal in the two following points), also a certain affinity with the text and its author[82]. This requirement also applies to the Catholic interpretation of the Bible,

---

[79] 1Cor 2,1. Cf. 1Cor 4,1 (cit. in the previous note); Mk 4,11 (// Mt 13,11 // Lk 8,10): "the mystery of the kingdom of God". Consider also: 1Cor 13,8-13 ("Ex parte enim cognoscimus et ex parte prophetamus... Videmus nunc per speculum in aenigmate..."); Eph 3,18-19 ("... and comprehend with all the saints what is the breadth and length and height and depth, and to know the love of Christ which surpasses all knowledge..."); Rom 11,33-34 ("O the depth of the wealth, the knowledge and the science of God! How inscrutable are his judgements and inaccessible his ways..."; cf. Wis 17,1: Μεγάλαι γάρ σου αἱ κρίσεις καὶ δυσδιήγητοι, "difficult to explain").

[80] VATICAN II, *DV* § 8 (*EB* 680): "Ecclesia..., volventibus saeculis, ad plenitudinem divinae veritatis iugiter tendit". On the need for study, given the transcendence of the object, cf. LEO XIII, *PrD* (*EB* 108); PIUS XII, *DaS* (*EB* 554): "... in Divinarum Litterarum campo, nunquam satis exculto, nunquam exhausto". On the promotion of biblical studies, cf. LEO XIII, *PrD* (*EB* 82 and ff.); PIUS X, Apostolic Letter *Vinea electa* (7 May 1909; *EB* 282 and ff.); BENEDICT XV, Encyclical Letter *Spiritus Paraclitus* (15 September 1920; *EB* 441. 480); PIUS XII, *DaS* (*EB* 538, at the end); VATICAN II, *DV* §§ 23. 24. 26 (*EB* 703. 704. 708).

[81] This axiom, which goes back to JEROME (*Epistola 49, ad Pammachium*, 17; CSEL 54, 381; PL 22, 507), is repeatedly cited in the magisterial documents of the last century, e.g.: LEO XIII, *PrD* (*EB* 106); BENEDICT XV, *SpP* (*EB* 487); PONTIFICAL BIBLICAL COMMISSION (Pius XII), *Letter to the Bishops of Italy* (*EB* 525).

[82] To understand music, you have to have a musical ear, to understand poetry, you must have a poetic soul, to understand law, you have to have juridical sensitivity; and so on. Those who are closed within the shell of their own narcissism are precluded from any form

and so indispensably as to demand a special interpretative *virtus*. Faith in the true divinity of the Bible, in fact, requires that the interpreter enjoy a kind of concord with the divine, that he hold therefore an adequate spiritual endowment. To understand the words of man, one must be endowed with the spirit of man; to understand the words of God, one must be endowed with the Spirit of God[83].

Thus the Church's appeal to interpret the sacred Scriptures in the Spirit, without ever separating interpretation from prayerful contact with the divine[84].

(c) *The requirement of exegesis.* To interpret *any text* faithfully, it is necessary to pay attention to and care for its original meaning, that which was intended by its author. In order to faithfully interpret *ancient texts*[85] – often passed down to us in a fragile condition, written in dead languages

---

of faithful interpretation, that is, any interpretation carried out in morality. Cf. PLATO, *Ion*, 531ab.

[83] VATICAN II, *DV* § 12 (*EB* 690), with reference to BENEDICT XV, *SpP* (*EB* 469) and to JEROME, *In Gal.* 5,19-20 (PL 26, 417A); INTERNATIONAL THEOLOGICAL COMMISSION, *Ip*, B, I, 2 (*EB* 1206); C, I, 3 (*EB* 1215). In 1Cor 2,9-15, Paul writes: "It is written: "What the eye has not seen, what the ear has not heard, what has never entered into the heart of man, these things God has prepared for those who love him" [Is 64,3; Jer 3,16; Sir 1,10]. But God has revealed them to us through the Spirit. For the Spirit scrutinizes everything, even the depths of God. Who knows human things except the spirit of the man which is in him? So too, no one has known the things of God except the Spirit of God. We however have not received the spirit of the world but the Spirit which comes from God, to know the things which God has given us... Man, with his psyche, [ψυχικὸς ἄνθρωπος: "the psychical man"; the Vulgate translates: *animalis homo*], does not perceive the things of the Spirit of God; for him they are folly, and he is not able to understand them because they have to be discerned spiritually (πνευματικῶς). The spiritual man instead (ὁ πνευματικός) can judge everything, while he can be judged by no one". See also: Gen 40 and 41; Qoh 8,1; Dan 2 (especially v. 45); and, above all, Dan 5.

[84] VATICAN II, *DV* § 25 (*EB* 705); INTERNATIONAL THEOLOGICAL COMMISSION, *Ip*, B, I, 2 (*EB* 1207). One might perhaps ask: "But is it then only believers, who have received the Spirit with their baptismal incorporation in Christ, who are able to interpret the Bible?". It is a pertinent question. For the answer, see below, at 2.3, a.

[85] If I am here limiting myself – in connection with the specific object under examination and to give greater emphasis to my argument – to discussing *ancient* texts only, this is not done with the intention to restrict the need for *exegetical* interpretation exclusively to this type of texts alone. On the contrary, I would hold that my considerations, to some degree and in a way, can be valid for recent texts as well, above all for those with recognized relevance for the current times, as is the case for those texts described *lato sensu* as "didactic" and/or normative.

or in languages that differ from the living ones, composed according to stylistic criteria dissimilar to those familiar to us, fragmentary testimonies to worlds that are more or less extinct –, something more is needed; what is required is *exegesis*[86], that is, a *scientific* study. Indeed, it is not possible to arrive at the proper and original sense of this type of texts, without subjecting them, with the aid of the appropriate techniques, to a historical-critical analysis, that pores over text, language, literary form, purpose and functions, author, addressees, contextual and cultural conditions, and historical circumstances. Here, the requirement of faithfulness translates into the requirement of exegesis.

This requirement also applies, in full, to the Catholic interpretation of the Bible. In fact, the Church believes not only in the true divinity of the Scriptures but also and additionally, as we have seen above, (in 1.1, b), in their true and inseparable *humanity* (it is faith in their "theandric" nature). The Bible is not "Word" of God in its pure state, in its absolute transcendence (if it were, it would remain absolutely impervious for us). Rather, it is Word of God "incarnated" in truly human words; a Word, therefore, historicized and inculturated (and this is how it becomes accessible to us, albeit only partially). This scriptural "incarnation" of the divine Word took place in well-determined times and places of a distant past. Not only in the eyes of reason, but also in the eyes of faith, is the Bible ancient record of a historical and ancient Revelation. As such, it cannot be understood except by understanding the concrete humanity, historicity and culture of the writings that compose it. Faithfulness to the divine letter of the text must, thus, translate, first of all, into faithfulness to its ancient human letter, and

---

[86] The term goes back to the Greek word ἐξήγησις, "explanation, (authoritative) interpretation" (from ἐξ-ἡγέομαι, "lead out", "guide", "control", "explain", "interpret"), which is used in connection with the specialist interpretation given by the ἐξηγηταί (= "exegetes") of the law (especially of sacred law, *fas*) (cf. DEMOSTHENES, *Contro Evergos*, XLVII, 68-71; ISAIOS, *The succession of Kiron*, VIII, 39; PLATO, *Euthyphro*, 4cd; *Laws*, 631a), as also of poetic writings (cf. PLATO, *Cratylus*, 407a). The modern use, which employs the term to refer to the scientific search for the original sense of a text, is obviously not found in the literature of ancient Greece (there being no such practice at that time). However, it is consonant with the ancient usage. One notes, in particular, that the meaning is "drawn out", "extracted" (ἐξ-ήγησις), with attention to fidelity, not "put in", "introduced" (εἰσ-ήγησις) at will, and that it is a function (one that is public and juridically binding) performed by experts. In the NT, only the verbal form ἐξηγέομαι appears (Lk 24,35; Jn 1,18; Acts 10,8; 15,12.14; 21,19), referring to the explanation/interpretation of events or realities, the divine sense of which is revealed.

the faithfulness to the intention of the divine Author must translate into faithfulness to the intention of its ancient human authors[87]. The interpreter is required to examine the individual biblical writings in their authentic text and to seek their original meaning by setting each in its historical context (linguistic, literary, cultural, economic, social, political, ideological, religious)[88]. In other words, he must carry out an exegetical enquiry; an enquiry that remains constantly open to new and better advances, an enquiry that no one can ever presume to end, declaring it concluded or closed *motu proprio*[89].

It goes without saying that, by its very nature, exegesis is the task of specialists, of *exegetes*; biblical exegesis is the task of biblical exegetes, of *biblical scholars*. It follows – like it or not –, that the faithful use of the Bible by those who are not specialists in biblical exegesis is necessarily (and duly) dependent on exegetical interpretation by biblical scholars.

The Catholic hierarchy, throughout the extended era of the Counter-Reformation culminating in the attack on modernism, strenuously resisted the scientific approach to the sacred Scriptures[90]. In this last century [the XXth century, *ed.*], however, the Church has gradually come to recognize its necessity, to the point of encouraging it within its rank[91]. Even if – it needs

---

[87] Vatican II, *DV* § 12 (*EB* 688). Earlier: Pius XII, *DaS* (*EB* 552-553); later: John Paul II, *Dtc* § 5 (*EB* 1244).

[88] Pius XII, *DaS* (*EB* 557); Vatican II, *DV* § 12 (*EB* 689).

[89] Even the Catholic hierarchy seems to have become aware of this. John Paul II, *Dtc* § 8 (*EB* 1247), writes: "L'étude des conditionnements humains de la parole de Dieu doit être poursuivie avec un intérêt sans cesse renouvelé". He is echoed by Cardinal J. Ratzinger, "Preface" to *IntB* (*EB* 1259): "Cette étude [that of the Bible] n'est jamais terminée; chaque époque doit de nouveau, à sa manière, chercher à comprendre les Livres Saints". We shall return to this theme later, in 2.3.

[90] The same Leo XIII, who is credited for the opening of the Bible to scientific study, indicates, among the things which no Catholic should doubt, "eam esse divinorum naturam Librorum, ut ad religiosam illam, qua involvuntur, obscuritatem illustrandam subinde non valeant hermeneuticae [understood as: exegetical] leges, verum dux et magistra divinitus data opus sit, Ecclesia [understood as: hierarchical magisterium]" (Apostolic Letter *Vigilantiae* [= *Vig.*], 30 October. 1902; *EB* 141; cf. *PrD*, *EB* 108).

[91] With the Apostolic Letter *Vigilantiae* [= *Vig.*] (30 October 1902) (*EB* 142), Leo XIII decisively approved (*"Nobis vehementer probantibus"*) the cultivation the critical method by Catholic scholars (*"artis criticae disciplinam... excolant"*). Since then, there has been a succession of increasingly explicit and well-reasoned pronouncements in this area. See: Pius XII, *DaS* (*EB* 538-569; especially 548 and 560, but the whole Encyclical is a defense of the scientific study of the Bible); Vatican II, *DV* § 12 (*EB* 688-689); Pontifical Biblical Commission, *IntB*, I, A, Proemium (*EB* 1275): "Sa juste compréhension [of sacred Scrip-

to be acknowledged – the official magisterium of the Catholic Church has yet to resolve some thorny theoretical issues, legacy of the doctrinal constructions created for the inauspicious battles of the past, and has yet to initiate a consonant magisterial practice, that is, one that respects the role of biblical exegesis that has now been recognized[92].

(d) *The requirement of hermeneia.* To interpret faithfully *any text*, it is necessary to pay attention to and devote care for not only its original sense but also its current sense; more precisely, it is necessary to ensure that the sense intended by the author is kept intact as it passes from its original predicatory context to the reader's present receptive context. In order to faithfully interpret (ancient or recent) *texts* that, broadly speaking, we can qualify as *didactic* and/or *normative* – namely, all those texts which are recognised as having a theoretical and/or practical value for the present –, something more is required; *hermeneia* is also required[93], that is, the verification of the effective correspondence between original meaning and

---

ture] non seulement admet comme légitime, mais requiert l'utilisation de cette méthode [the historical-critical method]"; JOHN PAUL II, *Dtc*, especially §§ 7 and 8 (*EB* 1246-1247).

[92] We shall return to these unresolved doctrinal nodes below, in 2.3. For a series of examples showing the scant consideration that the Catholic hierarchy reserves to biblical exegesis and its advances in its magisterial practice, see my essay "L'istituto famigliare dell'antico Israele e della Chiesa primitiva", *Anthropotes* 13 (1997) 109-174 (especially part III, pp. 160-174).

[93] It is usual to speak of "hermeneutics". However, there is more than one reason that has prompted me not to use this term, and to suggest that it should not be used in the area of disciplines dealing with, or otherwise relating to, scientific interpretation. *First*: "hermeneutics" is used with a hundred different meanings; its use condemns us to ambiguity and leads to misunderstandings. *Second*: in one of its more common meanings, "hermeneutics" stands as a synonym of "interpretation": its practice or theory. But then, this "practice of interpretation" or "theory of interpretation" is often reduced, concretely, to the sphere of developing a sense for today, and possibly only for "the today" of the "hermeneut" in question; the other sphere, that concerned with the search for the original sense (exegesis), is neglected, if not outright excluded, as if it were not equally essential, on a par with the former sphere, to the "phenomenon" currently called "interpretation". *Third*: "hermeneutics" is often understood as meaning the elaboration of a *current* sense; but, while it is held that interpretation must begin with the search for the original sense, its necessary completion consists in the elaboration of an *actualized* sense (and not simply of any kind of *current* sense). *Fourth*: "hermeneutics" recasts in modern language the ancient Greek term ἑρμηνευτικός - ή -όν, an adjective (one speaks, for example, of ἡ ἑρμηνευτικὴ τέχνη, "the hermeneutical science", that is, the science of translating, of explaining), derived from nouns of the same root. In fact, to indicate the corresponding action, the Greek language had in fact the terms ἑρμηνεία e ἑρμήνευσις; to indicate the corresponding agent, the terms

present meaning, and, if this is lacking, the sapiential elaboration of an 'actualized' sense[94], in such a way that the original meaning intended by the author can be maintained intact in the *hic et nunc* of the reader/user. It is clear that the greater the temporal, cultural and historical distance of the original context (that in which the text in question was written) from the present setting (that in which it is received and is to be followed), the greater the need for *hermeneia*.

This requirement also applies, and in the highest degree, to the Catholic interpretation of the Bible. In fact, the Church believes that its sacred books, written in a past that is, in many ways, remote to us, are (ought to be) perennially valid; it believes that they maintain (ought to maintain) *in saecula saeculorum* their kerygmatic-didactic value for the "today" of every human being and their normative value for the "today" of the faith and morals of believers. The Word of God was not "incarnated" ("historicized", "inculturated") in the ancient Scriptures solely for the benefit of the generations of the biblical times and places, but also and equally for the

---

ἑρμηνευτής and ἑρμηνεύς. Accordingly, there is no reason to use as a noun the adjective formed precisely from these nouns.

For all these reasons, I prefer to speak: (*a*) of "interpretation", to indicate the interpretative process as a whole; (*b*) of "exegesis", and, correspondingly, of "exegete" and of "exegetical", to indicate the first stage of interpretation, that concerned with the scientific search for the original sense (it is the "exegetical" interpretation); (*c*) of "hermeneia", and, correspondingly, of "hermeneut" and of "hermeneutical" (with initial "h", as the transliteration of the harsh spirit of these Greek terms demands, and as is fitting, in order more clearly to mark the distance from current uses), to indicate the second stage of interpretation, the one concerned with sapientially developing the original sense (known through exegesis) into an actualized sense (it is the "hermeneutical" interpretation).

[94] The Latin maxim *in claris non fit interpretatio* seems to be in need of rethinking, once it is placed within the terminological and semantic frame of the previous note. The supposed "clarity" (*in claris*) – let us say, of a text – may concern the original sense (*de sensu originario*), and in that case there would be no need to devote scientific research to it (*non fit interpretatio exegetica*); however, the need remains, as far as the original meaning is concerned, to pay attention, to not take such "clarity" for granted, to not stop at the words of the text, but instead to seek out the writer's intention. All this is already an act of "interpreting" (*sed fit interpretatio*). The supposed "clarity" (*in claris*) may then concern the current sense (*de sensu actuali*); and in this case, there would be no need to proceed to its actualization (*non fit interpretatio* hermeneutica]; the need still remains, also as far as the current meaning is concerned, to pay attention, to not take such "clarity" for granted, to check whether the frame of reference which determines the original sense is so identical to the frame of reference that determines its current sense, that no actualization is required. And all this is also an act of "interpreting" (*sed fit interpretatio*).

benefit of the generations of all times and all places. In order to achieve this aim (of remaining the living Word of God), it has to be "dis-incarnated" ("de-historicized", "dis-inculturated") from its original human forms, those in which it was received, practiced and preached in the biblical world – which, insofar as they are human, are "imperfect and temporary"[95] –, as also from its subsequent forms, those in which it was received, practiced and preached in the various worlds crossed by the Church, and must be "re-incarnated" ("re-historicized", "re-inculturated") in new human forms, those in which it can and must be received, practiced and preached in the contemporary world; in one word, it has to be "actualized" and continually "re-actualized" again.[96] Therefore, the interpretation of the Bible, if it is intended to be faithful to the intention of the divine Author, cannot be limited to the exegetical work, to a scientific research on the sense of the original historical incarnation (the biblical one) of the divine Word. It must rather be prolonged *into* and be supplemented with a hermeneutical task, namely, with the dismission of the old incarnations of the divine Word (beginning with the biblical one) and with the theological elaboration of its ever new historical incarnations, so that the divine Word can remain at all times living in senses that are appropriately actualized to the present. As "ancient", the biblical books require exegesis; as "ancient" and simul-

---

[95] Discussing the books of the OT, VATICAN II, *DV* § 15 (*EB* 693), writes: "Qui libri, quamvis etiam imperfecta et temporaria contineant, veram tamen paedagogiam divinam demostrant". Obviously, this also applies to the books of the NT. "Imperfection" and "impermanence" depend on the constitutive theandricity, that characterizes the entire Bible. Cf. JOHN PAUL II, Apostolic Letter on the dignity and vocation of women *Mulieris Dignitatem* (15 August 1988), § 24. The true humanity of Scripture does not allow the biblical Word of God to remain valid *sicut exstat*, as such, for all times, for all cultures and in all circumstances. The human forms in which the Word of God is historically incarnated grow old and die. And once they are dead, they become lethal. Not the simple *repetition,* but rather the more complex *actualization* preserves the continuity and validity of the biblical Word. In order to *remain* within history, the Word is averse to being static; it demands to be advanced and, where necessary, surpassed (cf. A. TOSATO, *Economia di mercato e cristianesimo*, Roma: Borla, 1994, pp. 19-29 and 111-169) [reproduced in A. TOSATO, *Vangelo e ricchezza. Nuove prospettive esegetiche*, Dario Antiseri, Francesco D'Agostino, Angelo Petroni (eds.), Soveria Mannelli: Rubbettino, 2002; the references above are found respectively at pp. 256-262 and pp. 125-186].

[96] The work of actualizing of biblical hermeneia – to express ourselves with a mathematical formula – consists in solving for the unknown term of the following equation: *Pb: cb = X: co*. That is: the biblical Word of God (= *Pb*) is to the historical biblical context (= *cb*), just as the Word of God today (= *X*) is to the historical context of today (= *co*).

taneously always "valid for the present", they also require *hermeneia;* this requirement too, is perpetual.

It goes without saying that, by its nature, *hermeneia* is the task of specialists, of the *hermeneuts*; biblical *hermeneia* is the task of the biblical hermeneuts, of the *theologians*[97]. Whether we like it or not, it follows that the faithful use of the Bible by those who are not specialists in biblical *hermeneia* is necessarily (and duly) dependent on its hermeneutical interpretation by theologians, in addition to its exegetical interpretation by biblical scholars.

The official magisterium of the Catholic Church, which in the last century [the XXth century, *ed.*] has come to affirm the true humanity of the sacred Scripture, to approve of its historical-critical study and to acknowledge its historical nature, has lately also come to discover the need for it to be inculturated and brought into the present times[98]. In this regard, greater conceptual clarity and greater terminological precision still need to be achieved; next, the problem of the necessary consequences of these acquisitions needs to be addressed, both as to the correct way of using sacred Scripture and the correct value to be attributed to one's dogmatic heritage.

2.2 *The criteria of biblical interpretation*

The Catholic faith in the salvific purpose of the sacred books and their documentary, kerygmatic-didactic and preceptive-normative character – not as a general and abstract Word of God but rather as the Memorial of God (document of the Revelation and of the Covenant), Teaching of God

---

[97] Given the high degree of specialization demanded by modern sciences, it is unlikely that the same individual will be able to carry out the work of both exegesis and hermeneia in a truly competent way.

[98] JOHN PAUL II, *Dtc* § 15 (*EB* 1256-1257); PONTIFICAL BIBLICAL COMMISSION, *IntB*, II, A, 2; III, C; IV A and B; "Conclusion" (*EB* 1396-1401; 1473-1487; 1504-1527; 1555-1560). In an address to Italian biblical scholars (25 September 1970: *AAS* 62, 1970, pp. 618-619), PAUL VI exhorted them, in order to comply with "the need for a true faithfulness to the Word", to keep a *twofold faithfulness: faithfulness* to the Word that was incarnated in an ancient culture (therefore, correct exegesis) and *faithfulness* to the man of today, to whom the Word also wishes to make itself present, incarnating itself in his new culture (therefore, enlightened hermeneia). In this connection, see J. DUPONT, "Storicità dei Vangeli e metodo storico dei Vangeli nella Costituzione dogmatica *Dei Verbum*", in AA.Vv., *A venti anni dal Concilio. Prospettive teologiche e giuridiche* (Quaderni di Synaxis, 1), Palermo: Ediz. OFTeS, 1984, pp. 51-73 (especially pp. 70-71). One will note how the passage cited here still lacks the distinction between the competences and roles of exegetes and hermeneuts.

(both *kérygma* and *didaché*) and Law of God (both legislative Code and moral Code), functional to the salvation of humanity – leads even more the Church to conduct itself with the utmost faithfulness to the Bible. One alone is the Revealer, the Teacher, the Lawgiver, the *Kyrios* and the Saviour[99]; and certainly He saves through grace, but according to the instructions and laws, of which the Bible is Memorial and Ordinance.

The faithfulness owed to the Bible as Word of God in truly human words (to the Bible as a theandric text) binds the Church – as we have just seen (in 2.1) – to the necessity and duty of biblical interpretation, to carry out this interpretation in the Spirit, as well as to structure it in the double process of exegesis (search for and exposition of the original sense) and *hermeneia* (elaboration and exposition of an actualized sense). The faithfulness due to the Bible as written Word of the Revealer, Teacher, Lawgiver, *Kyrios* and Saviour (to the Bible as a text of a documentary, didactic and normative character ordered to salvation) further binds the Church to carry out its biblical interpretation following precise methodologies and directing its work to a precise purpose.

In fact, according to the testimonies of the NT, and in particular of the Gospels, Jesus[100] not only "interpreted"[101] the Scriptures himself, but

---

[99] Sole Revealer, cf. Jn 1,1.14.18; 3,11-13; sole Teacher, cf. Mt 23,8-12 and Jn 13,12-17; sole Lawgiver, cf. Mt 5-7; 11,28-30; Jn 13,34; 15,10.12.17; sole Kyrios, cf. 1Cor 8,6; 12,5; Eph 4,5; sole Savior, cf. Acts 4,12.

[100] In the many cases of interpretation and of diatribe about the interpretation of the Scriptures, attributed to Jesus in the Gospels, it is not easy to discern what is to be historically ascribed precisely to Jesus himself and what to his first followers. Moreover, with reference to our subject matter, it must be borne in mind that the Gospel traditions are the result of a process of transmission that has undergone three distinct stages: the first is that of Jesus' preaching to the Jews; the second is that of the oral and written retelling made by the Apostles to Jews and Gentiles; the third is that of the drafting of the Gospels, written by the three Synoptic evangelists for Greek-speaking Christian communities composed predominantly of Gentiles (the Fourth Gospel is probably to be ascribed to a further stage). Cf. PONTIFICAL BIBLICAL COMMISSION, Instruction *Sancta Mater Ecclesia (de historica evangeliorum veritate)*, *EB* 644-659. In this paper, it is not necessary to go into such controversial topics. Whether it be ascribed to Jesus, to the Apostles or to the Evangelists, what is important for us is the fact that this interpretative practice of the early Church, in as much as it is scriptural, has a value that is "canonical", rule-making, for the Church of all times.

[101] Examples, both for exegesis and for hermeneia, are provided further below. It is to be noted, as far as terminology is concerned, that in Jn 1,18 it is said that "no one has ever seen God", but that the "*monogenes (theos)*, who is in the bosom of the Father, he ἐξηγήσατο", that is "has expounded (him)", has reported (on him) (in all detail)"; for the meaning of the

also harshly denounced, regarding interpretation, both the "scribes" (οἱ γραμματεῖς, that is, οἱ νομικοί, the "doctors of the law")[102], and more generally his coreligionists, his fellow nationals (ἡ γενεὰ αὕτη, "this generation")[103]. Regarding the interpretation by both groups, He condemned not just their conclusions, but firstly their method and purpose.

Normative teachings about the criteria for the Church's biblical exegesis may be obtained from the dispute between Jesus and the scribes. It seems possible to gather them around the following three: (a) the wording of Scripture (that is, of the Law); (b) the intention of Scripture (that is, of the Law); (c) the intention of the Author (that is, of the Legislator). These three criteria are interconnected in an order of necessary progression: the first is functional to the second, and the second to the third.

(a) *The dictate of Scripture (of the Law)*. First of all Jesus clashes with the scribes over the fact that they at times, basing themselves on interpretative tradition, annulled the precepts of the Law[104]. "Why do

---

verb, cf. the only other occurrences of the term in the NT (Lk 24,35; Acts 10,8; 15,12.14; 21,19). Exegetical correctness requires that we avoid burdening the Johannine expression with a technical significance which is foreign to it. More significant, from the point of view of hermeneia, is the expression of Lk 24,27, in which it is said that Jesus διερμήνευσεν [cod. D: ἦν...ἑρμενεύειν] to the disciples of Emmaus ἐν πάσαις ταῖς γραφαῖς τὰ περὶ ἑαυτοῦ. Here we are properly in the area of biblical interpretation, and this is, in fact, an elaboration and explanation of an actualized sense (as will be clarified later). More generic, but nonetheless instructive, is the testimony of Acts 14,12: ἐκάλουν τε τὸν Βαρναβᾶν Δία, τὸν δὲ Παῦλον Ἑρμῆν, ἐπειδὴ αὐτὸς ἦν ὁ ἡγούμενος τοῦ λόγου.

[102] The designation οἱ νομικοί (the interpreters of the Nomos=Torah=Law, quintessence of the Scripture; the current translation in English is "the doctors of the law"), preferred by Luke (see 7,30; 10,25; 11,45.46.52.53; 14,3), clarifies the role and the importance of the γραμματεῖς in the Jewish community in the time of Jesus. They were of course divided into various "schools" and various learnings. Jesus and the first Christian communities were in conflict with those of the Pharisaic school above all, and more specifically with those of the *bêt Hillel*.

[103] See, for example, Mt 11,16; 12,41.42; 23,36; 24,34. Jesus addresses "this generation" with expressions of harsh condemnation: it is a "wicked and adulterous" generation (πονηρὰ καὶ μοιχαλίς, Mt 12,39; 16,4); " incredulous and perverse" (ἄπιστος καὶ διεστραμμένη Mt 17,17) and so on.

[104] In the Gospels, the Pharisees elevate themselves as defenders of the παράδοσις τῶν πρεσβυτέρων (Mk 7,3.5; Mt 15,2). Paul attests that he was, before his conversion, an ardent upholder of the traditions of the Fathers, περισσοτέρως ζηλωτὴς ὑπάρχων τῶν πατρικῶν μου παραδόσεων (Gal 1,14). Even extra-biblical Jewish sources attest that Pharisaism had elevated its own oral Tradition to an interpretive norm for Scripture. To legitimize this, the Pharisees argued that this tradition corresponded to a part of the Sinaitic revelation that Moses had transmitted exclusively in oral form, and which the Fathers had then handed

you transgress the commandment of God for the sake of your tradition?[105] So, for the sake of your tradition, you have made void the Word of God". Interpretative custom, a human elaboration, cannot and must not allow anyone to obliterate (*ob-literare*) the dictate of the Law, divine precept[106]. To begin with, all the faithful (interpreters not excluded) must accept those commandments (great and small) that God has seen fit to transmit in written form, such as they are, and must then put them into practice and teach others to put them into practice[107].

Hence the insistence of the Catholic official magisterium on the duty to interpret the sacred books according to their literal sense[108]; hence too the

---

down from generation to generation, without interruption, up to them (cf. bShab 31a). JOSE-PHUS, *Antiquitates*, 13, 297, writes: "The Pharisees have imposed many laws on the people which they derived from the Tradition of the Fathers (ἐκ πατέρων διαδοχῆς), not written in the Law of Moses". For other important testimonies, cf. E. SCHÜRER, *The History of the Jewish People in the Age of Jesus Christ*, ed. G. VERMES and F. MILLAR, vol. II, Edinburgh: Clark, 1979, pp. 389-391.

[105] Mt 15,3.6: Διὰ τί καὶ ὑμεῖς παραβαίνετε τὴν ἐντολὴν τοῦ θεοῦ διὰ τὴν παράδοσιν ὑμῶν; ...ἠκυρώσατε τὸν λόγον τοῦ θεοῦ διὰ τὴν παράδοσιν ὑμῶν (similarly reported by Mk 7,8.9.13; note the insistence on "your"; in Mk 7,8 and Col 2,8 it is specified: παράδοσις τῶν ἀνθρώπων). Here, the question and condemnation are illustrated by the interpretation given by the scribes to the commandment: "Honour your father and your mother" (Ex 20,12 // Deut 5,16), cited in v. 4 along with the relevant penal norm: "Whoever curses his father or mother is to be punished with death" (Ex 21,17 // Lev 20,9). The interpretative tradition which Jesus indicts was that which exempted children from the obligation to provide economic support to their needy parents, if they had declared *qorban*, "holy offering" (for the cult), in the same amount (Mt 15,5-6). This is only one example: "And of similar (interpretations) you make many" (Mk 7,13). For example, in relation to the norms on cultic purity (Mt 15,1-2.10-20 // Mk 7,1-7.14-23).

[106] Jesus accuses his opponents of hypocrisy and repeats to them the prophecy of Is 29,13: "This people honours me with its lips / but its 'heart' [= mind] is far from me. / They worship me in vain / teaching doctrines which are human precepts" (Mt 15,7-9 // Mk 7,6-7).

[107] Mt 5,19. Already in the writings of the Qumran community, there seems to be, regarding the interpretation of the Law, an anti-Pharisaic polemic analogous to that raised by Jesus. To reaffirm the priority of Scripture over tradition, the Community appealed to the norm of Deut 19,14 (cf. Deut 27,17; Job 24,2; Prov 15,25; 22,28; 23,10; Hos 5,10): "You shall not move 'the borders' [= the border stones] of your neighbour, placed by your ancestors..."; these "border stones" – they taught – are the scriptural norms. See CD 1,16; 5,20; 19,15-16; 20,25. Pertinent observations on the theme are offered by M. KISTER, "Some Aspects of Qumranic Halakhah", in *The Madrid Qumran Congress*, ed. J. Trebolle Barrera and L. Vegas Montaner, vol. 2, Leiden: Brill, 1992, pp. 574-576.

[108] PIUS XII, *DaS*: "Exegeta catholicus... germanam ipsam Sacrorum Librorum sententiam reperiat atque exponat. Quo in opere exsequendo ante oculos habeant interpretes

refusal to consider Tradition as an autonomous source of the divine Revelation[109], and the recognition of the limits of the scriptural interpretation of the Fathers[110].

---

sibi illud omnium maximum curandum esse, ut clare dispiciant ac definiant, quis sit verborum biblicorum sensus, quem litteralem vocant" (*EB* 550). The "literal" sense is that "ex verbis ipsis expressus" (*EB* 555). Additionally, in the writings of the Ancient Near East (like the Bible), the literal sense should not be presumed to be obvious: "Exegeta non quasi in antecessum statuere potest, sed accurata tantummodo antiquarum Orientis litterarum pervestigatione" (*EB* 558). One should not sacrifice the literal interpretation, as some would claim, in favour of a self-styled "spiritual" or "mystical" interpretation. The genuine spiritual sense is that which is present in the letter of the text, not that which is added to it from the outside (*EB* 552-553). Cf. JOHN PAUL II, *Dtc* § 5 (*EB* 1244); PONTIFICAL BIBLICAL COMMISSION, *IntB*, I, A, 4; II, B, 1; III, B, 3 (*EB* 1287; 1405-1411; 1471).

[109] Cf. above, 1.2, fn. 21. The analogous relationship between *Ius divinum* ("Divinum ius in scripturis divinis habemus", AUGUSTINE, *Tract. in Joh. ev.*, VI, 25.26; *apud Decretum Gratiani*, D. 8, can. 1) and *consuetudo* may shed light on the correct relationship between Scripture and Tradition. On this relationship, the *Decretum Gratiani* (I Pars, Distinctio 8) provides various and concordant *auctoritates*. For example, can. 6 ("Veritate revelata, consuetudinem sibi cedere oportet") records the following passage of AUGUSTINE (*De baptismo*, III, 8 e ss.): "Qui contempta veritate presumit consuetudinem sequi, aut circa fratres invidus est et malignus, quibus veritas revelatur, aut circa Deum ingratus est, inspiratione cuius ecclesia eius instruitur. Nam Dominus in Evangelio: "Ego sum", inquit, "veritas"; non dixit: Ego sum consuetudo. Itaque veritate manifestata veritati cedat consuetudo. Revelatione ergo facta veritatis cedat consuetudo veritati, quia et Petrus, qui circumcidebat, cessit Paulo veritatem predicanti. Igitur cum Christus veritas sit, magis veritatem, quam consuetudinem sequi debemus, quia consuetudinem ratio et veritas semper excludit".

[110] The COUNCIL OF TRENT (*DSS-II*; *EB* 62), repeated by VATICAN I (*DF*, cap. II; *DS* 3007; *EB* 78), had established the "unanimous consent of the Fathers" as a criterion for the correct interpretation of Scripture (we shall return to this later, in 2.3, fn. 213). Hence the custom of the Catholic magisterium of identifying in the doctrine of the Fathers, in the ecclesiastical interpretative tradition – and not in the Scripture! (cf. above, fn. 107) –, the boundary stones placed by the "ancestors"; cf., e.g., CONGR. S. ROM. ET UNIV. INQUISITIONIS, *Lam.* (*EB* 190); BENEDICT XV, *SpP* (*EB* 453 and 474); already GELASIUS, Letter *Licet inter* (year 490), in H. DENZINGER, *Enchiridion Symbolorum*, ed. 31, Barcinone etc.: Herder, 1960, n° 161. A fair reconsideration of the authority of the Fathers in exegetical matters was undertaken by PIUS XII, *DaS* (*EB* 554-555). This recognized that "interdum eruditione profana et linguarum scientia minus instructi erant, quam nostrae aetatis interpretes"; the Catholic exegete "egregie *iuvari poterit* sollerti illorum operum studio" (my italics). Along the same lines, VATICAN II (cf. *DV* §§ 12 and 23; *EB* 690 and 703) and the PONTIFICAL BIBLICAL COMMISSION (*IntB* III, B, 2; *EB* 1453-1463). In the *Decretum Gratiani* (I Pars, Distinctio 9, can. 3), it is established that the writings of the Fathers "Scripturis canonicis… deserviunt", arguing from a passage from the Prologue of the *De Trinitate* of AUGUSTINE: "Noli meis litteris quasi canonicis scripturis inservire [Roman edition: deservire]. Sed in illis et quod non credebas cum inveneris, incunctanter crede: in istis autem, quod certum habebas, nisi certum intellexeris, noli firme tenere".

(b) *The intention of Scripture (of the Law)*. Jesus clashes with the scribes, again, over the fact that, while they did refer to the text of the Law at times, they then stopped short at its letter (and even *infra litteram*)[111], neglecting the *ratio Legis* (whether the *ratio* of the individual norms[112], or the *ratio* of the legislative system, that is their coherence with the cardinal precepts – the Ten Commandments and, in the final instance, the commandment of the love of God and neighbour[113] –, of which the more detailed laws are

---

[111] The rabbinic tradition did not disdain to make its case even on the basis of single alphabetical letters (the *'ôtîjôt min ha-tôrah)*, cf., for example, bB.K. 63b; bJeb. 68b. One of the proponents of this interpretation *infra litteram* was R. Akiva (first half of the II century A.D.). The contemporary R. Ishmael, his antagonist, countered with the principle: *dibberah torah kelašon benê 'adam*, "the Torah is expressed in human language" (jJeb VIII 8d; jNed I 36c; bBer 31b; bShab 63a; bSahn 56a; 64b).

[112] This is the case, for example, of Jesus' diatribe against the scribes' interpretation of perjury. The rule of the Law prescribed: "Do not perjure but fulfill your oaths with the Lord" (Lev 19,12; Num 30,3; Deut 23,22; cf. Ex 20,7). The "oath" mentioned here is that issued by making a vow. In order to avoid uttering the name of God (a non-existant precept, instead the product of a "literalist" interpretation of Ex 20,7, the commandment that, if understood correctly according to its "mind", precisely prohibited perjury!), the faithful swore by the Temple, or the Altar, or something else similar and equivalent to "God". Here the scribes, with their interpretation of the norm, came to the aid of the unwary who, repenting of their vows, sought justification not to keep them: "If one swears by the Temple, it does not count, but if one swears for the gold of the Temple, he is bound... If one swears by the Altar, it does not count, but if he swears by the offering which is on the altar, he is bound" (Mt 23,16.18). Jesus is outraged at such interpreters: "Blind guides!..Foolish and blind!..." (Mt 23,16-22). Other examples of "literalist" interpretation condemned by Jesus are found in Mt 5,21-26 (about the "You shall not kill") and in Mt 5,27-30 (about the "You shall not commit adultery"); also in Mt 5,31-32; 19,3-9 (about the legislative "concession" of repudiation).

[113] Jesus reduces the whole of the Law and the Prophets *ad unum*, to the first and highest commandment: Mk 12,28-34 // Mt 22,34-40 // Lk 10,25-28. Paul does the same: Gal 5,14; Rom 13,8-10. James speaks of νόμος βασιλικὸς: Jas 2,8. This was already so for HILLEL (end of the I cent. B.C.): bShab 31a. The procedure followed by Jesus in his dialogue with the rich (young) man is instructive (provided that the Gospel account – Mt 19,16-22 and parallels – is not utilized for a functional reading of the traditional Catholic teaching about the "evangelical counsels" and the "state of perfection"; cf. TOSATO, *Economia di mercato e cristianesimo* (above fn. 95), pp. 63-67 and 90-96 [also in A. TOSATO, *Vangelo e ricchezza. Nuove prospettive esegetiche*, cit., fn. 39 above, pp. 281-283 (fn. at pp. 304-305; and pp. 437-440 (fn. at pp. 454-457)].

only intended to be concrete manifestations)[114]. In so doing, they frustrated the laws, wholly or in part, annulling or at the very least reducing their real preceptive scope. "You blind guides, straining out the gnat and swallowing the camel"[115]; *summum ius, summa iniuria*[116].

In line with this teaching, the official Catholic magisterium encourages the exegete not to stop at the mere letter of the text but to research its meaning, in particular paying attention to the typical expressions and forms of writing of the Ancient Middle East to which the hagiographers and those whom they were addressing belonged[117].

(c) *The intention of the Author (of the Lawgiver)*. Finally, Jesus clashes with the scribes over the fact that they did, at times, go so far as to consider the *ratio Legis* but without respecting its spirit, without being able to trace the Law back to the *mens Legislatoris*. "The sabbath [understand: the commandment of sabbatical rest] was made for man, not man for the sabbath"[118]; "Is it lawful on the sabbath to do good, or to do evil? To save a life or to let it

---

[114] See, for example, Jesus' reproach of the scribes for their way of interpreting the norms on cultic purity (also condemned, in this respect, in Mt 15,10-20 // Mk 7,14-23) and those relating to the payment of tithes (Mt 23,23-24).

[115] Mt 23,24.

[116] CICERO, *De officiis*, I, 10. See in this regard the comprehensive study of comparative ancient law by D. DAUBE, "*Summum ius – Summa iniuria*", in IDEM, *Studies in Biblical Law*, New York: KTAV Publ. House, 1969, pp.190-313.

[117] BENEDICT XV recalls the teaching of Jerome: "Quae in verbis insit significatio et sententia, docet esse inquirendum, quia "de Scripturis sanctis disputanti non tam necessaria sunt verba quam sensus" " (*SpP*; *EB* 485). PIUS XII recalls a statement of Thomas: "Ipse Angelicus Doctor hisce verbis animadvertit: "In Scriptura divina traduntur nobis per modum, quo homines solent uti"" (*DaS*; *EB* 559; cf. 560, and above, fn. 108). The II VATICAN COUNCIL also returned to the subject, *DV* § 12 (*EB* 689).

[118] Mk 2,27 (2,23-28 // Mt 12,1-8 // Lk 6,1-5): Τὸ σάββατον διὰ τὸν ἄνθρωπον ἐγένετο καὶ οὐχ ὁ ἄνθρωπος διὰ τὸ σάββατον. The commandment is found in Ex 20,10-11 // Deut 5,12-15; cf. Ex 23,12. The *ratio* of this norm is, clearly, the sabbatical rest; but its *spiritus*, the mens *Legislatoris*, is, equally clearly, the good of the living, beginning with human beings. Incidentally: the intention of the Lawgiver (= spirit of the law) appeared in the very letter of the commandment on the sabbatical rest. See, in particular, Deut 5,14.

perish?"[119]; "Mercy I want, and not sacrifice"[120]. The observance of the letter and of the reason (of the intrinsic and direct intention) of a law can translate, for various circumstances, into a violation of its purpose, that is the ultimate intention of the Lawgiver who issued it. When this does happen, the Law is elevated from a means to an end. There is the semblance of great respect for the Law; in reality, this is a radical perversion of the Law and betrayal of the Lawgiver's intention[121]. We are thus faced with a blasphemous form of of interpretation, all the more odious by the fact that the faithful are subjected to unbearable burdens as if they were willed by God himself [122]; and "transgressors" are condemned as sinners[123].

The official Catholic magisterium does not hesitate to indicate the search for the *mens* of the author (of the human authors and in them of the

---

[119] Mk 3,4 (3,1-6 // Mt 12,9-14 // Lk 6,6-11;14,1-6): Ἔξεστιν τοῖς σάββασιν ἀγαθὸν ποιῆσαι ἢ κακοποιῆσαι, ψυχὴν σῶσαι ἢ ἀποκτεῖναι; cf. Lk 13,10-17; 14,1-6: here too there is a *reductio ad absurdum*, with a call to common sense, made *ad personam*, Mt 12,3-5; Lk 13,15-16; 14,5.

[120] Mt 12,7: Ἔλεος θέλω καὶ οὐ θυσίαν. This is a citation of *Hos* 6,6: *kî ḥesed ḥafaṣtî welo'-zevaḥ*. In Mt 9,13 (9,10-13), Jesus appeals to this same principle to justify his own conduct – judged by the Pharisees to be *contra legem* – of eating with "publicans and sinners" (people who did not observe the Pharisaic norms about food purity and were therefore contaminated and contaminating); a justification provided by condemning an erroneous interpretation of the Law.

[121] This phenomenon was already well known in the classical, Greek and Roman, world, which resolved it in terms of ἐπιέικεια and of *aequitas*. ARISTOTLE, *Rhetoric*, I, 13 (1374 a 26 - b 22); *Nicomachean Ethics*, V, 10 (1137 a 31 - 1138 a 3); CICERO, *De oratore*, I, 56 (240); 57 (244); *De officiis*, III, 16; CELSO, in D. 1.1.1 pr. The Aristotelian tradition is followed by THOMAS, *Summa Theologiae*, II-II, q. 120, a. 1, in corpore. For a historical survey, with extensive bibliography, see O. BUCCI, "Per una storia dell'equità", *Apollinaris* 63 (1990) 257-317 [the valuable treatise is now published as a volume: O. BUCCI, *Il principio di equità nella storia del diritto*, Napoli: Edizioni Scientifiche Italiane, 2000].

[122] Mt 23,4. Cf. Mt 11,28-30; Acts 15,10; Gal 5,1. Jesus' anger (ὀργή) at this type of interpreters is understandable, Mk 3,5. And no less understandable is the relief and joy of the crowd, in listening to Jesus' non conformist interpretation, Lk 13,17. Note that, on occasion, Jesus attributes his "violation" of the sabbath with the deliberate meaning of being a defiance and reproach of the "doctors of the law" and their interpretations of the Law. See for example the actions of Jesus in response to being reprimanded by the head of a synagogue, Lk 13,14-17.

[123] Jesus' disciples (Lk 6,2) and Jesus himself (Lk 13,14; Jn 9,16) are accused of a breach of the divine Law for their behaviour on the sabbath.

divine Author)[124] as supreme principle of (exegetical) interpretation, and to recognize that this *mens* aims solely at human salvation[125].

If the dispute between Jesus and the scribes provides us with normative teachings about the criteria of exegesis, then the other, broader and more radical, clash between Jesus and his co-religionists provides us with normative teachings about the criteria of *hermeneia*. These seem to amount to the following three criteria: (d) the newness of the gospel; (e) the needs of the times; and (f) the conditions of the individual peoples and individual persons. These three criteria are mutually complementary and inseparable.

(d) *The evangelical newness*. The clash between Jesus and his co-religionists arises from the request by the former and the refusal by the latter to recognize the "fulfilment" of the Scriptures (of "the Law and the Prophets") in the Gospel (as a historical event)[126]. At stake is the authentication of the Christian event as divine Revelation.

---

[124] Pius XII, *DaS* (*EB* 557): "Interpres igitur omni cum cura… dispicere enitatur, quae propria fuerit sacris scriptoris indoles ac vitae condicio, qua floruerit aetate, quos fontes adhibuerit sive scriptos sive ore traditos, quibusque sit usus formis dicendi. Sic enim satius cognoscere poterit quis hagiographus fuerit, quidque scribendo significare voluerit. Neque enim quemquam latet *summam interpretandi normam* [my italics] eam esse, qua perspiciatur et definiatur, quid scriptor dicere intenderit, ut egregie Sanctus Athanasius [*Contra Arianos*, 1, 54; PG 26, 123] monet: "Hic, ut in omnibus aliis divinae Scripturae locis agere convenit, observandum est, qua occasione locutus sit Apostolus, quae sit persona, quae res cuius gratia scripsit, accurate et fideliter attendendum est, ne quis illa ignorans, aut aliud praeter ea intelligens, a vera aberret sententia". Cf. Vatican II, *DV* § 12 (*EB* 688) and the references in fn. 81 in connection with the axiom *Non quid ipse [interpres] velit, sed quid sentiat ille, quem interpretatur*.

The *Decretum Gratiani* (II Pars, Causa 22, quaestio 5, can. 11), on the subject of oaths (establishing which are binding and which are not), cites this passage by an unknown author: "Certe noverit ille, qui intentionem et voluntatem alterius variis verbis explicat, quia non debet aliquis verba considerare, sed voluntatem et intentionem, quia non debet intentio verbis deservire, sed verba intentioni". God judges according to the intentions of the hearts, 1Cor 4,5; Rom 2,16.

[125] CIC (1983), can. 1752: "salus animarum suprema lex" (cf. above, fn. 18). The principles are good; the practice, as we unfortunately know, somewhat less so.

[126] Cf. Mt 5,17; Lk 24,44; Jn 19,30. The preachings of Jesus and the Apostles, like the New Testament writings later and in greater measure, are scattered with explicit and implicit references to the books of the OT, made with the aim of showing the correspondence between ancient promises and the new reality, inaugurated by the Christ. Cf. the expressions ὡς (καθώς, καθάπερ), γέγραπται (γεγραμμένον) and other similar ones.

In advancing his request, Jesus poses the need to proceed to an actualizing (innovative) interpretation of Scripture and to take the Gospel as a criterion for such actualization (innovation). In fact, the Gospel of Jesus introduces a newness, the radical newness, in the course of the history of divine Revelation[127]. As *novum*, it is not present as such in the Scriptures which are an expression of the *antiquum*. It is, however, present in them as *mysterion*[128]. Therefore, exegesis (the search for the pure, original sense of the texts) is not enough to find the Gospel in the (Judaic) Scriptures; *hermeneia* is needed. More precisely: it is necessary to relate the ancient Scriptures to the Christian event (to Jesus' evangelical proclamation, to His person, His passion, death and resurrection and to the gift of His Spirit), and to reread the former in the light of the latter. Only in this way are we able to understand the (Judaic) Scriptures as a "preannouncement" of the Gospel, and the latter as "fulfilment" (as perfecting and surpassing) of the former.

In posing the need for an actualizing interpretation of Scripture, and in putting forward His own Gospel as criterion of this actualization, Jesus is not advancing an anomalous claim. As we have seen above in 1.2, the

---

[127] The NT speaks repeatedly and in various ways of this newness (καινότης, καινός). We already mentioned it above (in 1.2), in connection with the "new Covenant" (Mt 26,28; Mk 14,24; Lk 22,20; 1Cor 11,25; 2Cor 3,6; Heb 8,8.13; 9,15; cf. Heb 12,24) and the "new commandment" (Jn 13,34; 1 Jn 2,7.8). There are many other occurrences: "newness of life" (Rom 6,4), "newness of spirit" (Rom 7,6), "new man" (Eph 2,15; 4,24; cf. 1Cor 5,7-8: "unleavened bread"), "new creature" (2Cor 5,17; Gal 6,15), "new wine" (Mt 26,29 and parallels; cf. Mt 9,17 and parallels; Jn 2,1-11), "new wineskins" (Mt 9,17 and parallels), "new garment" (Lk 5,36), "new teaching" (Mk 1,27; Acts 17,19), "new heaven and new earth" (2Pet 3,13; Rev 21,1), "new name" (Rev 2,17; 3,12), "new song" (Rev 5,9; 14,3), "new Jerusalem" (Rev 3,12; 21,2). New writings arose to give voice and testimony to this newness, some of which will merge into what would later constitute the "New Testament".

[128] In Rom 16,25-26, Paul speaks of his εὐαγγέλιον, of his κήρυγμα about Jesus Christ, as "revelation of the mystery (ἀποκάλυψις μυστηρίου) kept secret for endless ages (χρόνοις αἰωνίοις σεσιγημένου), but now manifested (φανερωθέντος δέ νῦν) ...". Cf. Mt 13,34-35; 1Cor 2,7.10; Col 1,26-27; 2,2; Eph 3,5.9-11; 1Pet 1,20. The writings of the Old Testament had indeed foretold the future divine intervention in favour of His people, but they had done so predominantly with triumphalist and miraculist inflections. Keeping to the original meaning of these texts, it is not possible to find a full correspondence between the messianic "promises" of "Law and Prophets" and the proclaimed "fulfilment" of the Gospel (it is lacking, above all, in relation to the outcome of the messianic endeavour: the "promise" spoke even of political success; while the "fulfilment" shows the failure in this respect: "Let Christ, the King of Israel, come down now from the cross so that we may see and believe", Mk 15,32).

Scriptures are the testimony of the Revelation of the living God, of his progressive intervention in human history. Thus, even leaving aside the explicit promises of the prophets, they foretell the continuation of *magnalia Dei* in the future by the sole fact that they celebrate the *magnalia Dei* of the past. The openness to (better: the tension towards) the *novum* of the divine work is something congenial, inherent in them[129]. "Is this not why you are wrong, that you know neither the Scriptures nor the power of God?"[130]. "Search the Scriptures", urges Jesus, "for they, too, bear witness to me"[131]. However, the Jews do not find this witness in the Scriptures: "it is not written!", or: "it is written differently!"[132]. And Jesus rebukes them,

---

[129] The exegetical study of Scripture highlights the presence of hermeneia in them; not as an accidental, marginal phenomenon, but as one that is substantial and central. So much so that it seems to be no exaggeration to claim that the Scriptures are themselves the product of an age-old, continual hermeneutical process. "Vetus Testamentum – writes the INTER-NATIONAL THEOLOGICAL COMMISSION., *Ip*, B, I, 1 (*EB* 1203) processus est interpretationis constanter novae et constantis relectionis; solummodo in Iesu Christo suam intepretationem invenit eschatologice definitivam". One may perhaps go even further, on the basis of 2Pet 1,20, if this passage is understood with correct exegesis (and not, as is wrongly done, even in the document just cited, in B, I, 2; *EB* 1206; for this criticism, see below, fn. 183). The prophecies (and, by analogy, this remark applies for all Scriptures) are the fruit of inspired hermeneia, an interpretation of the unexpressed "Word of God" within the concrete reality of a historical context. The "canonicity" of the interpretation-actualisation of the written Word of God finds here further and more radical confirmation.

[130] Mk 12,24: Οὐ διὰ τοῦτο πλανᾶσθε μὴ εἰδότες τὰς γραφὰς μηδὲ τὴν δύναμιν τοῦ θεοῦ. Here, the rebuke falls on the misunderstanding of Scripture with reference to a specific point of doctrine. However, the error can be fundamentally ascribed to an error in interpretative method (equating "interpretation" and "exegesis") and, before that, to a mistaken view of Scripture (the identification of Scripture with Revelation). Cf. above, in 1.2.

[131] Jn 5,39: Ἐραυνᾶτε τὰς γραφάς... καὶ ἐκεῖναί εἰσιν αἱ μαρτυροῦσαι περὶ ἐμοῦ· Cf. Jn 1,45; 5,46; 12,16.41; Lk 18,31

[132] Cf. Jn 1,46; 7,41-43.52. IGNATIUS, *Ad Philadelphienses*, 8,2: "I heard some say: "If I do not find (it) in the ancient writings (ἐν τοῖς ἀρχείοις), I do not believe in the Gospel". And when I said to them: "it is written", they replied: "That is the question!". But, for me, 'ancient writings' (ἀρχεία) is Jesus Christ...". Here we see clearly the serious interpretative problem, already faced by the first Christians. It is legitimate to wonder if everyone had the intellectual strength to resolve it as Ignatius does, with hermeneia, or whether, instead, apol-ogetic zeal led them down another path, namely to "fix" some of Jesus' biographical details, so as to make their own Messiah more concordant with the messianic prophecies and thus make it easier to overcome the difficulty of recognising in him the "fulfilment" that had taken place. This hypothesis is supported by some passages of the NT. See, for example, Jn 1,45-46.52; 7,40-43; Mk 12,35-37 and parallels. We would be facing a phenomenon of fundamentalism *ante litteram*. Instead of adapting the ancient Scriptures to the new Revela-

applying to them (with *hermeneia!*) the prophecy (ἡ προφητεία) of Isaiah: "You will hear but not understand, you will see and not perceive. For the 'heart' [= the mind] of this people has hardened, their ears have become hard and they closed their eyes so as not to see with their eyes, not to hear with their ears and not to understand with their 'heart', and be converted for me to heal them"[133]. Their error lies in not distinguishing between Scripture and Revelation, and in presuming to trace the Christian newness, as it is, back to the ancient Scriptures and thus to the previous phase of Revelation; whereas they should instead do the exact opposite[134]. "Their minds have hardened. To this day, in fact, that same veil [with which Moses covered his face, Ex 34,33.35] remains, unlifted, when they read the Old Testament, because it is in Christ that it is eliminated"[135]. Jesus has to act as a hermeneut for his own followers: "Fools and slow of 'heart'... And beginning with Moses and all the Prophets he explained (διερμήνευσεν) to them what in all the Scriptures referred to himself... Then he opened their mind to the intelligence of the Scriptures"[136].

It is not a question of patching the old garment with a new piece of cloth or of filling old wineskins with new wine. Instead, it is a matter of stitching

---

tion, by means of hermeneia, the new Revelation is adapted at certain points to the ancient Scriptures. Weak faith – it is human – needs and seeks to be propped up; fearful of progress, it tends to be contented with what it has ("No one who drinks the old wine desires the new for he says: The old is good!", Lk 5,39). It would not be scandalous if the hagiographers had now and then come to the aid of their weaker brothers (cf. below, at point f).

[133] Mt 13,14-15 (with citation of Is 6,9-10). The passage continues (vv. 16-17) expressing approval for those who find the fulfilment of the "old" in the new: "But blessed be your eyes for they see and your ears for they hear. In truth I tell you: many prophets and just men desired to see what you see and did not see it, and to hear what you hear and did not hear it".

[134] Cf. IGNATIUS, *Ad Philadelphienses*, 6,1. The Greek Fathers call interpreting the scriptural texts in a purely literal way ἰουδαΐζειν "judaize" ("ἰουδαϊκῶς "according to the Jewish way"), and ἰουδαϊκός, "Jewish", the purely literal sense resulting from such interpretation (cf. G.W. LAMPE, *A Patristic Greek Lexicon*, Oxford: Clarendon Press, 1961, p. 674). Not incorrectly, since, in their eyes at least, the Jews showed that they were not able to actualize in Christ the prophetic promises. Translating in our language, the Jews were observing the requirement of exegesis, but not that of hermeneia (or even if observing it, they did not assume the Gospel of Christ as criterion of their actualisation).

[135] 2Cor 3,14. Here the use of "the Old Testament" (ἡ παλαιὰ διαθήκη) appears for the first time to indicate the Scriptures relating to the Revelation centred on the Covenant between Yhwh and Israel.

[136] Lk 24,25-26.44-45. Equally, Philip acts as hermeneut for the Ethiopian pilgrim grappling with the interpretation of the prophecies of Isaiah (Acts 8,26-35); Paul (e.g. Acts 17,1-3.11) and Apollo (Acts 18,24.28) act as hermeneuts for the Jews.

an entirely new garment and of preparing new wineskins[137]. In fact, every actualization is, to some extent, an innovation; to perform it, it is necessary to have the spirit of the newness which compels the actualization and constitutes its criterion. The Christian actualization of Scripture is evangelical innovation; to perform it, it is necessary to have the Spirit of the Gospel, the Spirit of Christ[138]. The newness is radical; it requires an actualization that is radical innovation.

From its very beginnings, therefore, the Church has carried out hermeneutical interpretation, of which the newness of the Gospel was both the motive and the criterion. The magisterium of the Church, even recently, never ceases to recall with Augustine that the New Testament *latet* in the Old and the Old Testament *patet* in the New[139], and it rightly urges to carry out the necessary hermeneia assuming Christ as its criterion[140]. However, it might perhaps be opportune today to take a small step forward and recommend practising hermeneia in a linear and transparent

---

[137] Cf. Mk 2,21-22 // Mt 9,16-17 // Lk 5,36-38. Less radical but still oriented in a hermeneutical sense is Mt 13,51: "For this [for having understood the parables of the kingdom] every scribe who has become a disciple of the kingdom of heaven is like a master of a house who takes from his treasure things new and things old". – Once one has passed, in Christ, from old to new (cf. 2Cor 5,17), it is necessary to guard oneself from turning back (Gal 1,6; 4,8-11; cf. 2Pet 2,20-22).

[138] 1Cor 2,6-16; Jn 14,26; cf. Jn 7,37-39; 16,13.

[139] VATICAN II, *DV* § 16 (*EB* 694); cf. INTERNATIONAL THEOLOGICAL COMMISSION., *Ip*, B, I, 2 (*EB* 1206, with a lacuna in the Latin text); PONTIFICAL BIBLICAL COMMISSION, *IntB*, III, C, 1 (*EB* 1477). Commenting on the fear shown by Israel in *Ex* 20,19, AUGUSTINE (*Quaestiones in Heptateuchum*, 2, 73; PL 34, 623; CSEL 28, III, 3, p. 141) recognized that it is well founded to attribute to the OT *potius* fear, to the NT love, "quamquam et in Vetere Novum lateat, et in Novo Vetus pateat". This is an elegant way of saying that the Gospel is found in the books of the OT as *mysterion* only, cf. *DV* §§ 15 and 17 (*EB* 693 and 695). By contrast, the circular sentences used by *DV* § 16 and by *Ip*, B, I, 2 are convoluted and in need of deciphering. On the one hand, it is said: "Libri Veteris Testamenti... in Novo Testamento significationem suam completam acquirunt et ostendunt" (*DV* § 16) and "it is necessary to interpret the OT in the light of its fulfilment in the NT" (*Ip*, B, I, 2). This is correct if understood with reference to hermeneutical interpretation, but wrong if understood with reference to exegetical interpretation. On the other hand, it is said: the books of the OT "illud [NT] illuminant et explicant" (*DV* § 16) and "the NT is to be understood in the light of the Old Testament promises" (*Ip*, B, I, 2). This is correct if understood with reference to exegetical interpretation, but wrong if understood with reference to hermeneutical interpretation.

[140] INTERNATIONAL THEOLOGICAL COMMISSION, *Ip*, B, I, 2 (*EB* 1206): "Ex eo [= Christo] et in eum omnes Veteris et Novi Testamenti affirmationes in sua interna sunt intelligendae unitate"; C, I, 3 (*EB* 1215): "Theologica Scripturae interpretatio a Iesu Christo Scripturae

manner. The modern mindset, which commendably loves scientific precision and historical correctness, cannot appreciate and even struggles to understand the poor custom of Christian interpreters (biblical scholars and theologians) of surreptitiously actualizing the Scriptures, that is, their practice of actually doing *hermeneia,* but producing *eisegesis* and then presenting it as *exegesis* (this may have been appropriate in the time of the Fathers, but it is no longer so in our time)[141]. There is a need, in this regard, to better order theory and practice, clearly distinguishing between *exegesis* and *hermeneia*, banning *eisegesis*, while reserving the tasks that belong to *exegesis* for *exegetes* to perform, according to the criteria and techniques of their science, and reserving the tasks that belong to *hermeneia* for *hermeneuts* to perform, according to the criteria and techniques of their art[142].

(e) *The requirements of the times.* The clash between Jesus and his coreligionists on hermeneia (the need to do it and how to do it) is further manifested in the accusation directed by the former against the latter of not paying due attention to their own times. At stake is the ability to perceive the Revelation of God that is manifested in the dynamic fabric of a concrete historical reality; and therefore also the ability to adapt the teachings

---

centro procedere debet"; section C, I, 4 (*EB* 1217) is entitled and discusses "De Scripturae centro christologico tamquam criterio".

[141] Hermeneia cannot be done at the expense of the text and its exegesis but can instead be done on the basis of the results of exegesis. The sacred text must be respected, and so must the exegesis, which has to be carried out according to its proper criteria. It is no longer possible today to actualize, either by altering the letter of the text (historical-textual criticism exists!), or by altering its meaning through translation (historical-philological critique and historical-literary criticism exist!), or by advancing anachronistic explanations (historical-ideological criticism and historical-theological criticism exist!). Actualization is a requirement of biblical interpretation (cf. above, 2.1, d), but it must be carried out according to its own criteria and along the lines (with the technique) of the equation suggested in fn. 96.

[142] The PONTIFICAL BIBLICAL COMMISSION, in *IntB* III, C ["La tâche de l'exégète"], 1 ["Orientations principales"] (*EB* 1475), writes: "Le but de leur travail [of Catholic exegetes] n'est atteint que lorsqu'ils ont éclairé le sens du texte biblique come parole actuelle de Dieu. À cet effet, ils doivent prendre en considération les diverses perspectives herméneutiques qui aident à percevoir l'actualité du message biblique et lui permettent de répondre aux besoins des lecteurs modernes des Écritures". Exegetes are being asked to do hermeneia. To me this seems mistaken. Exegetes must be asked to carry out exegesis (and hermeneuts to carry out hermeneia). Mixing these functions together results in bad exegesis and bad hermeneia.

and the scriptural norms to the divine instructions and imperatives which emerge with the changing of the times. In the final analysis, what is at stake is the faithfulness to the living God, as well as to the Scriptures which are and wish to remain the authentic testimony of this living God.

If the contemporaries of Jesus are not able to recognize the *novum* of divine Revelation in the Gospel, nor therefore to deduce all the necessary consequences from this, it is also because they do not give due importance to the "present time" factor. "When you see a cloud rising in the west, you say immediately: Rain is coming, and so it happens. And when the south wind is blowing, you say: It will be hot, and so it happens. Hypocrites! You know how to examine (δοκιμάζειν, "test") the appearance of earth and sky, so how is it that you do not know how to examine (δοκιμάζειν) this time (καιρὸν τοῦτον)?"[143]. It is not enough to scrutinize the Scriptures. It is also necessary to scrutinize the times. It is, in fact, in the times that God reveals Himself; it is also in the times that God speaks. It is necessary to "scrutinize them" (subject them to "exegesis"), because they change (therefore the Word of which they are bearers also changes)[144] and because God reveals himself in them, not by means of extraordinary, heavenly signs – as the Jews would demand, who seek "a sign from heaven" (σημεῖον ἐκ τοῦ οὐρανοῦ) –, but rather by means of ordinary, earthly signs, the "signs of the times" (σημεῖα τῶν καιρῶν)[145]. Not through marvels in fact, does

---

[143] Lk 12,54-56: ...τὸ πρόσωπον τῆς γῆς καὶ τοῦ οὐρανοῦ οἴδατε δοκιμάζειν, τὸν καιρὸν δὲ τοῦτον πῶς οὐκ οἴδατε δοκιμάζειν. The *Gospel of Thomas*, § 91, offers a verb of equivalent value: πειράζειν, "test", "submit to testing". The verb used by Mt 16,2-3 is somewhat different: διακρίνειν, "distinguish", "discern".

[144] Not only for agnostics, but also for fundamentalists (perhaps more for the latter than for the former) does the maxim of Qoh 1,10 apply: *Nihil sub sole novum*. It is worth remembering, nonetheless, that Qoheleth knows very well how to distinguish between one time and another, between conduct fitting for one time and conduct fitting for another: "For everything there is a season / a time for every matter under heaven / A time to be born, a time to die. / A time to plant, a time to uproot. / A time to kill, a time to heal. / A time to destroy, a time to build. / A time to weep, a time to laugh. / A time to mourn, a time to celebrate. / A time to make love, a time to abstain from it..." (Qoh 3,1-5).

[145] Cf. Mt 16,1-4: Jesus reproaches the Jews, who ask him for a "sign from heaven [= from God]", as being, for such a request, "a perverse and adulterous generation"; and counters this with the "signs of the times", and then also the "sign of Jonah". The *Gospel of Thomas*, § 91, also connects Jesus' rebuke, for lack of attention to their own time, to a similar request. The insistence on being able to witness miraculous signs characterises the Jews' approach to the Christian proclamation (1Cor 1,22; cf. for example, Lk 11,29; 23,8; Jn 6,30).

God "speak" in the world, but through humble events[146]. By ignoring the signs of the times, Israel has missed its appointment with divine salvation and set itself out for disaster. Weeping for the ruin which looms over Jerusalem, Jesus accuses: "If only you too had recognized on this day (ἐν τῇ ἡμέρᾳ ταύτῃ) what was for (your) good; but now it has remained hidden from your eyes… you have not recognized the time of your visitation (τὸν καιρὸν τῆς ἐπισκοπῆς σου)"[147].

Jesus' accusation is addressed to fellow citizens of his generation. However, it contains a warning that is valid for all the generations of every nation, and a normative teaching permanently valid also for his disciples. Certainly, the *novum* of the time of Jesus Christ constitutes a historical *hapax* (a *unicum*)[148]; and it is, therefore, valid as a lasting criterion of Christian scriptural hermeneia[149]. But this *hapax* does not mark the end of times, nor does it block the course of human history, nor does it cause the multiform expression of the divine Word to cease within this course. Its advent therefore does not abolish the hermeneutical criterion of the

---

[146] This is the paradox of the way in which God reveals Himself in the world; cf. 1Cor 1,23-25.28; Mt 19,30. This contrasts strongly (and surprisingly) with the gospel narratives, rich with "signs from heaven". Even in connection with these narratives, it is legitimate to ask if the evangelists did not, for pastoral reasons and in the light of the post-Easter faith, shape their accounts on the basis of the constraints of the popular mindset concerning the divine and according to the narrative literary genre of the time. In addition to the passages examined here, this is suggested by Mk 8,11-12 (Τί ἡ γενεὰ αὕτη ζητεῖ σημεῖον; ἀμὴν λέγω ὑμῖν, εἰ δοθήσεται τῇ γενεᾷ ταύτῃ σημεῖον) and Mt 12,38-39 (+ 16,4) // Lk 11,29 (σημεῖον οὐ δοθήσεται αὐτῇ εἰ μὴ τὸ σημεῖον Ἰωνᾶ). The "sign of Jonah" seems to represent the first step on the road of concessions, made by the Christian hagiographers to the request to show "signs" comparable to the miraculous ones in the OT.

[147] Lk 19,41-44: Εἰ ἔγνως ἐν τῇ ἡμέρᾳ ταύτῃ καὶ σὺ τὰ πρὸς εἰρήνην νῦν δὲ ἐκρύβη ἀπὸ ὀφθαλμῶν σου, οὐκ ἔγνως τὸν καιρὸν τῆς ἐπισκοπῆς σου. To his contemporaries He intones the chant of the youngsters who complain to their playmates: "We played the flute for you and you did not dance; we intoned a lament and you did not weep. John came, who does not eat nor drink, and they said: He has a demon. The Son of Man came, who eats and drinks, and they say: Look, a glutton and a winebibber, a friend of publicans and sinners. But to Wisdom justice has been done by His works", Mt 11,16-19 (// Lk 7,31-35; here, the concluding sentence is partly different: "But to Wisdom justice has been done by his children").– To those challenging his disciples' failure to observe the fast, Jesus retorts: "Are the wedding guests able to fast while the bridegroom is with them? The days will come when the bridegroom will be taken away from them, and then they shall fast", Mt 9,14-15 (// Mk 2,18-20 // Lk 5,33-35).

[148] ἅπαξ: Heb 9,26.28; 1Pet 3,18; Jude 3.

[149] While the *antiquum* is τὸ καταργούμενον (*quod evacuatur*), the *novum* is τὸ μένον (*quod manet*), 2Cor 3,11. Cf. Jn 12,34; Heb 13,8; 1Pet 1,23-25.

signs of the times. Moreover: the Christian *novum* is a *hàpax paradothèn* (a *unicum traditum*)[150], the *efàpax* (the once and for all)[151] that is inserted into the course of human history and accompanies it, not as a dead letter (which kills), but rather as a living Spirit (which gives life)[152]; not as a petrified body of doctrines and norms, but rather as a dynamic principle in the Church and in the world (the leaven which raises all the dough). As the times evolve, it unfolds its inexhaustible potential and makes itself better known. Thus, it performs its stable and irreplaceable role as a hermeneutical criterion in that, it too, is continually subjected anew to the hermeneutical criterion of the signs of the times. The designation of Jesus Christ as the *Alpha* and the *Omega* gives rise to similar considerations[153]. Let us leave aside here the purely transcendental dimension, and instead consider the historical dimension. He is the *Alpha* in His first and completed advent, the *Omega* in His second and awaited advent. And it is for the intermediate time, the time of the pilgrim and preaching Church, that Jesus Christ launches his appeal: "Keep vigil"[154]. The Church's "vigilance" is to be directed, first of all, to the *Alpha* and the *Omega*, to the *unicum* of its past and its present, as well as at that of its future; but at the same time, it must also always be directed to the changing times of human history, to the signs that appear in them to communicate the divine Word and indicate the *Christus veniens*. Just as Israel lived a *fieri* toward the *Alpha*, so the

---

[150] Cf. Jude 3. Cf. Heb 12,27.28.

[151] ἐφάπαξ: Heb 7,27; 9,12; 10,10.

[152] Cf. 2Cor 3,6.17; 1Cor 15,45; Rom 7,6. Compared to the new Revelation, that which is received through and in Christ, Scripture (including the NT, testimony of the New Covenant) plays a less important role than it did in relation to the ancient Revelation, the one received through Moses (testimony of the Old Covenant). In fact, the New Covenant is centred on the gift of the *Spirit,* the Old Covenant on the gift of the *letter*. Cf. Jn 1,17; Rom 6,14; Gal 5,18.

[153] Ἐγώ εἰμι τὸ Ἄλφα καὶ τὸ Ὦ: Ap 1,8; 21,6; 22,13. Similarly, there should be no misunderstanding about the sense of expressions such as "the times are fulfilled", "fullness of times" and the like. They say that something irreversible has occurred, bringing one era to an end, but opening another.

[154] Γρηγορεῖτε: Mt 24,42; 25,13; 26,38.41; Mk 13,5.37 (ὃ δὲ ὑμῖν λέγω πᾶσιν λέγω· γρηγορεῖτε); 14,3.38; Acts 20,31; 1Cor 16,13; cf. Lk 12,35-40 (ἔστωσαν ὑμῶν αἱ ὀσφύες περιεζωσμέναι καὶ οἱ λύχνοι καιόμενοι); 41-48; 1Thess 5,1-8; Col 4,2; 1Pet 5,8; Rev 3,2.3; 16,15 (μακάριος ὁ γρηγορῶν). Ἀγρυπνεῖτε: Mk 13,33; Lk 21,36; cf. Eph 6,18. Νήψατε: 1Pet 4,7; 5,8; cf. 1Thess 5,6.8; 2Tim 4,5; 1Pet 1,13 (ἀναζωσάμενοι τὰς ὀσφύας τῆς διανοίας ὑμῶν νήφοντες τελείως); Rom 13,11-14 (καὶ τοῦτο εἰδότες τὸν καιρόν, ὅτι ὥρα ἤδη ὑμᾶς ἐξ ὕπνου ἐγερθῆναι, *et hoc scientes tempus*…).

Church lives a *fieri* toward the *Omega*. Just as the error of the Jews, who made themselves indifferent to the signs of the times, was to intend to enclose Christ (the *Alpha*) in the OT, so too would the Christians be in error if, making themselves in turn indifferent to the signs of the times, they intended to enclose Christ (the *Omega*) in the NT. Moreover, just as the people of Israel were given a "non-people" (the Church) as a providential sign of the times in order to awaken their jealousy and lead them to conversion[155], so the Church could be given another "non-people", in order to awaken it, if necessary, from its torpor (from the "spirit of torpor")[156] when it comes to hermeneia to be carried out with the criterion of the signs of the times.

It was precisely an evaluation of the times looming on the horizon, that of the apocalyptic vision common to their epoch, that led Jesus and his first disciples to formulate their singular and highly misinterpreted rules of conduct. And in fact: if God's intervention – the decisive one, marking with a single blow the end of the old aeon and the beginning of the new one – is at the gates, and with it national liberation from the Roman oppressor (not only the spiritual liberation of "souls"), then one must not, nor does it do any good to rebel for now, refusing to pay the tribute imposed by Caesar. Rather: "Render to Caesar what is Caesar's"[157]. If the kingdom of God is near, and with it his justice, then one must not, it is not the opportune time to oppose the wicked; "rather: if one strikes you on the right cheek, give him the other, too; to him who sues you to take away your tunic, let him have your cloak, too"[158]. If "time has now become

---

[155] Cf. Rom 10,19 (with a quotation of Deut 32,21: "I will make you jealous of a people which is not a people, I will make them angry with a foolish nation"); 11,11. Cf. Num 11,27-29; Mk 9,38-40.

[156] Cf. Rom 11,8: πνεῦμα κατανύξεως (quotation of Is 29,10: *rûaḥ tardemah*, "lethargy"). And see Deut 29,1-3.

[157] Mk 12,13-17 // Mt 22,15-22 // Lk 20,20-26; cf. Mt 5,43-46. The early Church reiterated the command to submit to the lawful authorities, to pay the tribute. This is the will of God. See: Rom 13,1-7; 1Tim 2,1-2; Tit 3,1-2; 1Pet 2,13-17. This submission is to be maintained even at the cost of trials, persecutions: 1Pet 1,6; 2,12.19; 3,13-17 ("blessed are you!"); 4,12-19 ("rejoice... blessed are you!"). Cf. Rev 13,7.9-10 (Whoever is destined for prison, to prison he goes! Whoever is destined to the sword, to the sword!).

[158] Mt 5,38-41; to correctly understand the meaning of these provisions, see Rom 12,17-21. In the same sense, Jesus proclaims as "blessed" the meek, the peacemakers and the persecuted: "for theirs is the kingdom of heaven [= the kingdom of God, that of imminent and decisive advent on the earth]", Mt 5,5.9.10.

short (ὁ καιρὸς συνεσταλμένος ἐστίν·, "has shrunk", "been reduced") and "the scene (the current order) of this world passes away" (παράγει γὰρ τὸ σχῆμα τοῦ κόσμου τούτου) with unparalleled upheavals and suffering[159], then one must, it is better to abstain for now from changing one's social status, especially family status, and to cease toiling in one's own professional activities: "let each remain in the condition in which he was when he was called. Were you a slave when called? Never mind; but even if you can gain your freedom, take advantage of your present condition instead... Are you bound to a wife? Do not seek to free yourself. Are you untied to a wife? Do not go to looking for one... let those who have wives live as though they had none..., those who buy as if they had no possessions"[160]; "Therefore, do not worry, saying: What shall we eat? What shall we drink? What shall we wear?.. Seek first the kingdom of God and his justice, and all these things shall be given to you in addition"[161]. The purported exceptionality of their time required the adoption of exceptional measures. The Law (the Torah) is subjected to a drastic actualization, to an astonishing adaptation: the validity of a large part of the Mosaic norms is suspended and a different transitional normative order comes into force in its place.

For those who know the Bible, there is nothing particularly new in this and, above all, nothing that contradicts the very nature of the Law (Torah). In fact, the exegetical study of the OT not only reveals well-known cases of exceptional measures taken in exceptional times (or considered as such)[162], but, what is more, it highlights the historical dimension of all the Israelite ("Mosaic") legislation. The "time" – the concrete, ever-changing historical conditions of the population and the assessments that were made on how to best address them – turns out to have had a decisive influence on the process by which its norms were adopted and how they evolved[163]. It seems fitting to speak of the Torah as of the product of

---

[159] On this aspect of the apocalyptic beliefs of early Christianity I have provided documentation in the article cited in fn. 92, pp. 151-153.

[160] 1Cor 7. Cf. Mt 19,10-12: the saying about the eunuchs "for the kingdom of heaven [= of God]", διὰ τὴν βασιλείαν τῶν οὐρανῶν.

[161] Mt 6,25-33 (// Lk 12,22-31).

[162] Cf., for example, Jer 16 and 29.

[163] To mention a few particularly striking examples: the sedentarization, the institution of the monarchy, the construction of the Temple as the fixed abode for the Ark, and the centralisation of the cult. There are those who do not accept the introduction of such innovations, not recognising them as expressions of the divine will. This is a refusal to read the signs of the times.

a centuries-old hermeneutical process. The procedure, which is clearly shown to be followed in extraordinary cases, offers us useful instructions about the procedure followed in the generality of cases. It instructs us, ultimately, on historicity as an intrinsic characteristic of the entirety of the Law. "Time" poses and imposes itself as its requirement and its criterion. If this is true for the moment of the institution and the subsequent transformation of the Law, it must be equally true throughout its actualizing interpretation, its being made operative in the present; and what is true for the OT, is true, albeit with the due differences, for the NT (always respecting the first hermeneutical criterion, 2.2, d).

It is by merit of [St.] John XXIII and of Vatican Council II that the Catholic magisterium has officially recognized the importance and affirmed the necessity of valuing the "signs of the times" as a hermeneutical criterion[164]. However, after the strong and exacting affirmations of the last [Vatican Council II, *ed.*] Council, only few and faint echoes have reached the ear.

---

[164] JOHN XXIII, Apostolic Constitution *Humanae salutis* (25 December 1961; this is the Constitution with which the Council was convened), *AAS* 54 (1962) 6; Encyclical Letter *Pacem in terris* (11 April 1963), *passim* (cf. A. TOSATO, cit. in fn. 95, pp. 138-143 (reproduced in A. TOSATO, *Vangelo e ricchezza. Nuove prospettive esegetiche*, cit., pp. 141-144 [footnotes at pp. 172-174]); VATICAN II, *GS* § 4 (but also, implicitly, §§ 11, 42 and, above all, 44) (*C.Vat.II - Doc.*, 1324; 1352; 1451 and 1453; 1460-1462); and again: *UR* § 4 (*C.Vat. II - Doc.*, 508); Decree *Apostolicam actuositatem* § 14 (*C.Vat.II - Doc.*, 967); Declaration *Dignitatis humanae* § 15 (*C.Vat.II - Doc.*, 1084); Decree *Presbyterorum ordinis* § 9 (*C.Vat. II - Doc.*, 1272). Cf. A. TOSATO, cit. in fn. 95, pp. 143-149; 166-167, fn. 88 (and in A. TOSATO, *Vangelo e ricchezza. Nuove prospettive esegetiche*, cit., pp. 145-148 [footnotes at pp. 175-177], 183-185, fn. 88); G. RUGGIERI, "Pour une herméneutique de Vatican II", *Concilium* (ed. franc.) 279, 1999, 13-26.

Given the scant attention currently being paid to the criterion explained above, it could be useful to listen again to the voices of some masters of the past. GRATIAN (*Decretum*, I Pars, Distinctio 29, can. 3 ("Pro diversitate locorum, temporum et hominum Scripturae intelligendae sunt") records the following passage of JEROME (*Comm. in Epistola ad Ephesios*, Proœmium): "Necesse est, ut iuxta diversitate temporum et locorum et hominum, quibus [Scripturae] scriptae sunt, diversas et causas et argumenta et origines habeant. Et quomodo B. Iohannes in apocalipsi sua septem scribens ecclesiis in unaquaque earum specialia vel vitia reprehendit, vel virtutes probat, ita et S. apostolus Paulus per singulas ecclesias vulneribus medetur illatis, nec ad instar imperiti medici uno colirio omnium oculos vult curare". Similar teachings are recalled in the two preceding canons. THOMAS, *Summa Theologiae*, I-II, q. 98, a. 2 ("Utrum lex vetus fuerit a Deo"), ad primum, distinguishes between *perfectum simpliciter* and *perfectum secundum tempus*, between *praecepta perfecta simpliciter* and *praecepta perfecta secundum conditionem eorum quibus dantur*.

(f) *The conditions of individual peoples and individual persons.* The clash between Jesus and his coreligionists, which brings to light the need to subject the Scriptures to hermeneia and to assume as its criterion, in addition to the Gospel, the signs of the times, is extended over time and extended in scope within the early Church, revealing a third hermeneutical criterion, that of ethnic and individual diversity. The need to actualize the Scriptures by also diversifying their normative scope according to ethnic differences emerges from the conflict between the evangelizers of the "Gentiles" (*imprimis* Paul, the Apostle of the "*Gentes*") and the evangelizers of the "Jewish-Christians". The former argue, against the latter, that the "Gentiles" (= non-Jews) must not be required to be circumcised as a condition for becoming Christians[165]. The Church endorses the former and officially adopts their view[166]. At stake is faithfulness to the Gospel as the message of universal salvation *in Christo* (and not *in the Law-Torah*).

Not imposing circumcision on the Gentiles who sought to become Christians was tantamount to not requiring them to become Jews: it was tantamount to not demanding that they renounce their nationality in order to adopt the Jewish one, nor that they abandon their own national law to submit to the Law of Israel[167]. It meant recognizing the ethnic privilege of the Jews, sanctioned by the Old Covenant, as lapsed. Membership of Israel and observance of its Law were no longer necessary for the acquisition of the divine promises. It was hence necessary, for all individuals (Jews and non-Jews) alike, to accept Christ, commit to the New Covenant, submit to the new Law, become part of the body of Christ, receive his Spirit. The result was that *Jewish* universalism (singularistic, nationalistic and imperialistic)[168] was dismissed and *Christian* universalism (pluralistic, transnational, "ecclesial", that is, based on the assembly of the people), emerged in its place[169]. The passage from one type of universalism to the

---

[165] 1Cor 7,17-18.20; Gal 6,12; Acts 15,1.5.24.

[166] Gal 2,1-10; Acts 15.

[167] Circumcision was obligatory for every male Jew on the eighth day after birth, Gen 17; Lev 12,3; Ex 12,44; Ezek 44,4-9. With this mark, he became incorporated into the people of Israel, inserted into the covenant with YHWH and subjected to the Torah. The bond between circumcision and observance of the Torah is recorded in the New Testament writings; cf. Acts 15,5.10; Gal 5,3; Rom 2,25.

[168] All nations would have been subjected by force to the Law and to the King of Israel.

[169] All individuals are invited to join, in communion with the same life-giving Spirit, the Community of the New Covenant in Christ.

other was legitimized through a reinterpretation of the Scriptures, which supplanted their traditional interpretation. "In truth I realize – confesses Peter bewildered to see that the Spirit had also descended on the Gentiles[170] – that *God makes no preferences of persons*, but whoever fears him and practices justice, whatever people he belongs to, is accepted by him"[171]. "Perhaps God – presses Paul, arguing with the Jewish Christians – is God of the Jews only? Is he not also the God of the Gentiles? Of course, of the Gentiles too! For there is but one God, who will justify the circumcised on account of their faith (περιτομὴν ἐκ πίστεως), and the uncircumcised through their faith (ἀκροβυστίαν διὰ τῆς πίστεως.)"[172]. There is one God, equally provident for all; and there is one Lord, who is equally munificent to all: "For the Scripture says: *Whoever believes in him will not be confounded*. For there is no distinction between Jew and Greek (οὐ γάρ ἐστιν διαστολὴ Ἰουδαίου τε καὶ Ἕλληνος); for the same Lord is Lord of all, rich toward all who invoke him. Indeed: *Whoever invokes the name of the Lord will be saved*"[173].

---

[170] Peter's phrase gives expression to the bewilderment which seized the whole of the first Christian community, constituted in Jerusalem and composed exclusively of Jews, when they acknowledged this earth-shattering innovation as a divine, incontrovertible "sign of the times". One may read the entire account of Acts 10-11,18. See, also, the *Letter to the Galatians*, which is a vivid documentation of the difficulties encountered by the Jewish Christians in translating their conceptual acquisitions and collective decisions into their consequent conduct. Cf. also IGNATIUS, *Ad Magnesios*, 10,3. Peter himself has to be publicly rebuked by Paul for his hypocritical conduct, Gal 2,11-14 (v. 14: πῶς τὰ ἔθνη ἀναγκάζεις Ἰουδαΐζειν).

[171] Acts 10,34-35: Ἐπ' ἀληθείας καταλαμβάνομαι ὅτι οὐκ ἔστιν προσωπολήμπτης ὁ θεός, ἀλλ' ἐν παντὶ ἔθνει ὁ φοβούμενος αὐτὸν καὶ ἐργαζόμενος δικαιοσύνην δεκτὸς αὐτῷ ἐστιν. That God makes no preferences among people is an axiom of the Jewish faith repeated several times in the Scriptures: Deut 17,10; 2Chr 19,7; Job 34,19; Sir 35,15; cf. Wis 6,7; Jubilees 5,16; Gal 2,6; 1Pet 1,17. The Christian reinterpretation, which transposes the axiom into the new context in order to legitimize the new doctrine, is found in Rom 2,10-11. "Justice" is no longer identified with the observance of the Mosaic Law, now relegated to being the ethnic law of Israel, but with the observance of the law of conscience (Rom 2,12-16), with the observance of the "commandments" as ethical principles common to all (1Cor 7,19). It was the belief of the Jews that they were "pure", "holy", while the Gentiles were instead "impure" (Acts 10-11,18, especially 10,28; cf. Mt 15,11), "sinners" (Gal 4,15). Circumcision was considered as a "purification", "sanctification".

[172] Rom 3,29; cf. Eph 2,11-22. See also the discourse on those who were truly "circumcised", Rom 2,25-29; cf. 4,9-12; Gal 5,15; 1Cor 7,19 (neither circumcision counts, nor uncircumcision, but observance of the commandments).

[173] Rom 10,11-13. Cf. Acts 10,36.43; Gal 5,6; Rom 9,33; 1Cor 8,6; 1Tim 2,5; Eph 4,5-6. The two Scriptural passages being reinterpreted are Is 28,16 and Joel 3,5.

This scripturalist reinterpretation (a radical actualization carried out by the early Church based on the two hermeneutical criteria laid out above, and recorded in the NT) provides grounds for the decision not to impose circumcision and the Torah on non-Jewish Christians. Yet, by doing so, this interpretation highlights (or, perhaps better, gives birth to) a third hermeneutical criterion, that of ethnic diversity. Respect for the practices and customs, the laws, the cultures of the different ethnic groups is hence imposed as a further requirement and norm for a pervasive and profoundly incisive adaptation of the Scriptures[174]. It requires, in fact, that the ancient Scriptures of the Jews, the whole of the Mosaic Law, regarded as the civil code of Israel, be considered non-applicable to the Gentiles,[175], and, as to the new Scriptures of the Christians, that their content be assessed in order to select and, if necessary, reserve for the Jews everything they may contain (intentionally or not) that is specifically Israelite.

This third hermeneutical criterion is not limited to requiring respect for ethnic diversities. Other, no less important differences must also be respected; first and foremost, those of social status and gender. Even before descending, independently, on the Gentiles (causing the bewilderment mentioned above), the Holy Spirit descended on the group of the Jews, followers of Jesus Christ, on men and women, on old and young, slaves

---

[174] It will be noted, therefore, that the Old Testament Scriptures (Law and Prophets) themselves, understood in the light of the Gospel and of the signs of the times, bear within themselves the principle of their extensive surpassing.

The specific national laws of each ethnic group, of course, remained intact for the convert to Christianity, as long as they did not contradict the law of Christ; but this was true both for the laws of the non-Jews and for the Law of the Jews. Cf. above, in 2.2, d, and here, below.

[175] With the exception of the commandments, which are the expression of the fundamental ethical principles, "natural law" or law of reason, spiritual heritage of the common human conscience (the *praecepta moralia*, to express ourselves with the category used by THOMAS, *Summa Theologiae*, I-II, q. 100), all the rest of the Mosaic precepts (the *praecepta caeremonialia* and the *praecepta iudicialia*, to continue expressing ourselves with THOMAS, *Summa Theologiae*, I-II, qq. 101-103; qq. 104-105), do not apply to them. In sustaining that the *praecepta iudicialia* (the norms of the ancient Law which regulated human relations) are no longer in force, Thomas writes: "Illa praecepta iudicialia disponebant populum ad iustitiam et aequitatem secundum quod conveniebat illi statui. Sed post Christum, status illius populi oportuit mutari, ut iam in Christo non esset discretio Gentilis et Iudaei, sicut antea erat. Et propter hoc oportuit etiam praecepta iudicialia mutari", I-II, q. 104, a. 3, ad tertium.

and free, without distinction, constituting the first Christian community. Peter could only acknowledge the event and see in it the fulfilment of the prophecy of Joel: "I will pour out my Spirit on every person. Your sons and your daughters shall prophesy, your young men shall have visions, your elders shall have dreams; even in those days, I will pour my Spirit on my menservants and my maidservants, and they shall prophesy ... who calls on the name of the Lord shall be saved"[176]. For Christians – Paul reminds the Galatians – there is neither Jew nor Greek, there is neither slave nor free, there is neither *male nor female* [Gen 1,27]; for you are all one in Christ Jesus"[177]. In relation to Christ and in Christ, all the differences, based on which all ancient legislation (Mosaic included) discriminated, conferring privileges on some to the detriment of others, instead command equal treatment. Therefore, the general principle recalled above, namely, that God makes no preferences among persons, applies even to the various human categories.

There is more. Diversity as a requirement and criterion of diversification for the actualization of the Scriptures not only relates to national belonging, social class and gender; it also relates to the individual conditions of each subject. Individuals have different capacities and possibilities; different are the times, the degrees and the modes of their maturing. Paul confesses that he feels in debt "to the Greeks as to the barbarians, to the wise as to the ignorant" and confesses: "I made myself weak with the weak, in order to gain the weak. I made myself all things to all (τοῖς πᾶσιν γέγονα πάντα), to save some at all costs. All I do for the Gospel, so that I may share it with them"[178]. "Every time you have done these things to only one of the least of these brothers of mine, you have done it to me"[179]. Paul's apostolic zeal finds in the earthly Jesus Christ (the one

---

[176] Acts 2,17-21; citation of Joel 3,1-5; Is 2,2; and cf. Acts 2,39: the promise of the gift of the Holy Spirit is "for you [Israelites]... and for all those who are far away, as many as the Lord will call". To understand the exceptional nature of this general effusion of the Spirit on *all* members of the community, it may be helpful to return to Num 11,16-17.24-30.

[177] Gal 3,28: οὐκ ἔνι Ἰουδαῖος οὐδὲ Ἕλλην, οὐκ ἔνι δοῦλος οὐδὲ ἐλεύθερος, οὐκ ἔνι ἄρσεν καὶ θῆλυ· πάντες γὰρ ὑμεῖς εἷς ἐστε ἐν Χριστῷ Ἰησοῦ. Cf. the already above-cited Rom 10,11-13 and Eph 2,11-22; and again: 1Cor 12,13 and Col 3,11.

[178] Rom 1,14; 1Cor 9,19-23. Cf. 2Cor 11,29; 1Cor 3,1-2; 10,31-33; Rom 14 and 15,1-13. It seems to me that the decision of the "Council of Jerusalem" (Acts 15), which was transitional in nature, requiring the Gentiles to observe certain Mosaic cultic norms, should be understood in this light.

[179] Mt 25,40 (25,31-46); cf. Mt 10,40-42; 18,5.

found in historical evidence and the one found in theological reflection on the incarnation) his model; in the glorified Jesus Christ (the one who has become a life-giving Spirit) his impetus ("No longer do I live, but Christ lives in me"[180]).

In relation to this last, very broad, sphere of application, the hermeneutical criterion of diversity seems to be specified in the criterion of "pastorality". In this regard, one would be tempted to speak of a fourth hermeneutical criterion. But perhaps it is more appropriate to see in "pastorality", modelled on and continuing that of Jesus Christ, the supreme biblical norm for the interpretation of Scripture. It, in fact, clarifies the *raison d'être* and the spirit of all the norms set out above and establishes the end towards which Christian interpreters must direct their work.

The most recent magisterial documents speak of the need for scriptural interpretation committed to actualizing in the sense of "inculturating" the biblical Word within the different cultural contexts of today[181]; but they do not go much further. There seems to remain ample space here for further study and more precise teachings.

2.3 *The forms of biblical interpretation*

Faith in the universal destination of the Bible leads us to recognize a *universal* call to interpret the Scriptures. If it is God's will that all human beings should be recipients-beneficiaries of the Bible, this means that it is also His will that all should be its interpreters and thus that all should have the proper capacities, duties and (basic) rights to interpret the sacred books.

However, faith in the universality of the destination of the Bible is coupled with faith in the multiplicity, variety and complementarity of the types of this destination. And this second truth leads us to recognize the existence of *multiple*, *varied* and *complementary* calls to its interpretation. If God, in fact, wanted that all human beings were to be recipients-beneficiaries of the Bible, but that Christians were also to be recipients-min-

---

[180] Gal 2,20; cf. Rom 8,10.

[181] JOHN PAUL II, *Dtc* §§ 15-16 (*EB* 1256-1258); PONTIFICAL BIBLICAL COMMISSION, *IntB*, above all in IV, A and B (*EB* 1504-1527). Similarly important is the acknowledgment of the pluralism present in the New Testament made by the INTERNATIONAL THEOLOGICAL COMMISSION., *Ip*, B, I, 3 (*EB* 1209); although it is still not enough. The pluralism which can be found in the New Testament seems to be a phenomenon that cannot be circumscribed to the area of "formulas".

isters; and that all Christians were to be ministers in as much as they were depositaries and witnesses, but that among them some were also to be ministers as divulgators, others as interpreters-exegetes, others as interpreters-hermeneuts and others, finally, as interpreters-judges of the hermeneia, this means that He also wanted there to be multiple, varied and complementary categories of interpreters, and therefore that each would have its own proper and distinct capacities, duties and rights to interpret the sacred books.

In addition, the conclusions reached above regarding the requirements of biblical interpretation, especially those of performing exegesis and hermeneia (cf. 2.1, c-d), and those regarding the criteria in accordance with which biblical exegesis and hermeneia are to be performed (cf. 2.2, a-f), bring us to distinguish among (but not separate) *qualified* interpretations and *common* interpretations, *qualified* interpreters and *common* interpreters.

Therefore, we can distinguish among the various forms of biblical interpretation (and corresponding various categories of interpreters) along the lines of the various types of destination of the Bible (and corresponding various categories of recipients), classifying them on the basis of the degree of their complexity and on the extent of their functionality. The forms of *common* interpretation (and the corresponding categories of *common* interpreters) are: (a) the *simple* form, that of any reader whether or not they are of the Christian faith; (b) the *devout* form, that of any faithful Christian; (c) the *vulgate* form, that of Christian preachers and catechists. The *qualified* forms of interpretation (and the corresponding categories of *qualified* interpreters) are: (d) the *exegetical* form, that of Christian biblical scholars; (e) the *hermeneutical and propositional* form, that of Christian theologians; (f) the *hermeneutical and judicial* form, that of the bishops. What are the capacities, duties and rights proper to each of these categories in relation to biblical interpretation?

(a) *"Simple" biblical interpretation.* All human beings, as recipients-beneficiaries of the Bible and urged by the Spirit to the obedience of faith[182], have the capacity and the duty to "interpret" the sacred books, in the sense that they can and must receive the message of salvation that God

---

[182] Cf. Rom 1,5; 6,16-17; 10,16; 15,18; 16,19.26. VATICAN I, *DF*, chapter III and the related can. 1 (*DS* 3008 and 3031).

addresses to them in these books[183]. At the same time, they also have the right (*vis-à-vis* the depositaries and witnesses), to have access to the Bible, translated into their own language and duly annotated[184] (in order to gain direct and certain knowledge of the biblical Word)[185], so that they may read

---

[183] It could be objected that, not having received with baptism the Holy Spirit, non-Christians are unable to "interpret" the Bible, "cum sacra Scriptura eodem Spiritu quo scripta etiam legenda et interpretanda sit" (VATICAN II, *DV*, § 12; *EB* 690); cf. above, in 2.1, b. Nonetheless baptism is the ordinary, but not the exclusive, form for the transmission of the Spirit. The Spirit blows where It wills (cf. Jn 3,8). In particular, it blows in the proclamation of the Gospel ("the words I have spoken to you are Spirit and Life", Jn 6,63; cf. Jn 3,34). In fact, the Gospel, by which God "calls people to his kingdom and his glory" (1Thess 2,12), is not mere human word but, through Him, divine Word, living and efficacious (1Thess 2,13; cf. Heb 4,12; 1Pet 1,23); Word of his grace (Acts 20,14.32; cf. Lk 4,22; Col 4,6; Eph 4,29). The preaching of the Gospel takes place through the movement of the Spirit and with communication of the Spirit (1Pt 1,23; cf. Acts 10,45-47; 11,15-17; 1Cor 2,10.12). "No one can say Jesus is Lord except under the action the Holy Spirit" (1 Cor 12,3). All this applies both to the oral proclamation and to the written proclamation (cf. VATICAN II, *DV*, § 21; *EB* 701). And, finally, some presence of God who is Spirit is to be recognized in every human creature, if it is true that "in Him we live, move and exist... For we are His offspring" (cf. Acts 17,28). The proclamation of the Gospel is in harmony with the deepest aspirations of the human heart (cf. VATICAN II, *GS* § 21, *C.Vat.II - Doc.*, 1384).

There is more. It could be objected, on the basis of 2Pet 1,20, that "no prophetic scripture is to be subject to private explanation, for [moved by the Holy Spirit spoke the Prophets] ...". But this is an unfortunate translation. The text has: πᾶσα προφητεία γραφῆς ἰδίας ἐπιλύσεως οὐ γίνεται. Jerome translates well: *omnis prophetia Scripturae propria interpretatione non fit*. As the context (1,16-21) enables us to understand, this is not said of the reader's interpretation, but the prophet's "interpretation" (*epìlysis*: "solution", "explanation") of the revelation received from God, and it affirms that this interpretation does not happen by means of the simple human activity of the prophet.

[184] VATICAN II, *DV*, § 22 (*EB* 702); § 25 (*EB* 706): what is prescribed in this regard in favour of the Christian faithful (cf. below, especially fn. 193) is to be considered prescribed also in favour of those who are not-yet Christians (cf. Rom 10,14-15.17). The means of the first Christian proclamation, as they were described by Luke in his account of the post-Easter Pentecost ("each one heard their own language being spoken", Acts 2,6.8), constitute for the Church a paradigm to which it must conform its evangelizing practices. One must also consider Paul's directives on the subject of "glossolalia" (1Cor 12,30; 14,5.13.26-28): no use is to be made of incomprehensible languages, unless there is someone who "interprets", that is, translates them into comprehensible language.

When we speak of a right of the "recipients" of the Bible to *read* it, to which corresponds a duty of the "depositaries" to make this reading possible, we intend to emphasize only the elementary right, without intending to exclude further rights, such as, for example, the right to scientific study.

[185] Cf. Jn 4,42. It is not surprising that, two millennia after the Christian Revelation and its first proclamation, living testimony (not always exemplary) and oral communication

it and find that this Word, lived by the Church, actually yields the fruits of salvation (to verify its validity)[186].

(b) *"Devout" biblical interpretation.* All Christians, as depositaries-witnesses (as well as recipients) of the Bible, endowed with the Holy Spirit (which is both Guide to the Truth and Strength for bearing witness)[187] and bound to take the sacred Scripture as nourishment and rule for their religious life[188], have the capacity and duty to "interpret" the sacred books[189], in the sense that they can and must meditate on them with devotion and assiduousness[190] in order to cultivate, verify, deepen, practice and ever more effectively bear witness to the Word which God has also written in their hearts[191].They have, at the same time, the right (*vis-à-vis* catechists,

---

(inevitably subject to gaps, obscurities, inaccuracies, and sometimes even contradictions) require the support of written communication.

[186] There is a right of humanity towards Christians to receive a living testimony of the Word of God. Consider the repeated, harsh rebukes that the Scriptures address to Israelites and Christians: by their conduct they give scandal, they provoke blasphemy against the name of God (for example: Is 52,5; Ezek 36,20-23; Rom 2,24; 14,13.16; 1Tim 6,1; Tit 2,5; 2Pet 2,2). Cf. VATICAN II, *LG* § 10 (*C.Vat.II - Doc.*, 311); *AG* § 37 (*C.Vat.II - Doc.*, 1216); *GS* §§ 19 and 21 (*C.Vat.II - Doc.*, 1375 and 1382).

[187] According to the promise (Ezek 36,26-27; Joel 3,1-5), God has poured out his Spirit on believers in Christ (Acts 2,16-21; cf. Rom 5,5; 8,9; 1Cor 3,16; 2Tim 1,14). And this Spirit, according to the promise (Is 54,13; Jer 31,34; cf. Jn 6,45), teaches all things: "the anointing [of the Holy Spirit] which you have received from Him [= Jesus Christ] remains in you, and you have no need for anyone to teach you; but as his anointing – which is true, not mendacious – teaches you about all things, just as it has taught you, so remain firm in Him" (1Jn 2,27; cf. 1Jn 2,22); "the Spirit of Truth… will lead you into all the Truth" (Jn 16,13). The same Spirit infuses the strength necessary to fulfil the mandate of giving witness (Mt 10,18-20; Jn 15,26-27; Acts 1,8; 2Tim 1,6-8; cf. Acts 4,8.31; 6,10). With the Spirit, every believer has received his own particular charisma (cf. below, footnotes 229 and 243). Cf. JOHN PAUL II, *CCC* § 91.

[188] VATICAN II, *DV*, § 21 (*EB* 701): "Ipsa religio christiana sacra Scriptura nutriatur et regatur oportet". In the same paragraph, Scripture is spoken of as "bread of life", "supreme rule of faith", "pure and perennial source of spiritual life".

[189] S. CONGR. PRO CLERICIS, *Directorium catechisticum generale* (11 April 1971; *AAS* 64, 1972, pp. 106-110), § 14 (*EB* 719): "Ecclesia sacrarum Scripturarum custos et interpres, ab eis docetur, assidue meditando et magis magisque penetrando earum doctrinam…"; "Ecclesia Spiritu animata ipsam [sacram Scripturam] interpretatur".

[190] Col 3,16: "Let the word of Christ dwell in you abundantly"; VATICAN II, *DV* § 22 (*EB* 702): "Christifidelibus aditus ad sacram Scripturam late pateat oportet"; cf. *DV* § 25 (*EB* 705); JOHN PAUL II, *CCC* §§ 131 and 133.

[191] "Cultivate", cf. Mt 13 (the Parables of the Sower and of the Tares); "control", cf. Gal 2,1-10 (Paul subjects his own Gospel to testing); "deepen", cf. above, in 2.1, regarding

biblical scholars, theologians and bishops) to not have the Bible taken away from them[192], but instead on the contrary to have it continually promoted and explained to them with adequate aids[193].

---

transcendence and mystery; "practice", cf. Jas 2,22-25; "bear witness", cf. above, fn. 187, and again 2Cor 3,18; 4,2.6; "written in their hearts", cf. Jer 31,31; 2Cor 3,3 and the passages relating to the Spirit, inner Teacher, cited in fn. 187; cf. the fine passage of the INTERNATIONAL THEOLOGICAL COMMISSION, *Ip*, C, II, 1 (*EB* 1219).

[192] In past centuries, starting as early as the XII century (INNOCENT III, Letter *Cum ex iniucto*, 12 July 1199: *DS* 770-771; PROVINCIAL COUNCIL OF TOULOUSE, 1229, can. 14: LABBÉ, *Sacrosancta Concilia*, XIII, Venezia 1730, col. 1239), there was a succession of increasingly restrictive measures by the Catholic hierarchy in matters of translation, publication, sale, purchase, possession and reading of sacred Scripture, backed by heavy criminal sanctions for transgressors. From the period of the Counter-Reformation onwards, until relatively recent times (the true turning point came only with PIUS XII, *DaS*; *EB* 549), the Bible remained in practice subtracted from use by the Catholic faithful. Decisive in this regard are the prohibitions (and related sanctions) issued with the various editions of the *Index librorum prohibitorum*, especially the Roman editions of 1559 (PAUL IV), of 1564 (the "*Regulae Tridentinae*", confirmed by PIUS IV) and of 1596 (CLEMENT VIII), for which see the monumental *Index de livres interdits*, ed. J.M. DE BUJANDA (and others), voll. VIII and IX, Sherbrooke-Genève: Centre d'Études de la Renaissance - Librairie Droz, 1990 and 1994, and the rich study of G. FRAGNITO, *La Bibbia al rogo. La censura ecclesiastica e i volgarizzamenti della Scrittura (1471-1605)*, Bologna: il Mulino, 1997; further bibliography can be found in M. INFELISE, *I libri proibiti*, Roma-Bari: Laterza, 1999. Papal vigilance over the application of these prohibitions was maintained in the XVIII and XIX centuries, as testified by, for example: CLEMENT XI, Constitution *Unigenitus Dei Filius* (8 September 1713), against the Jansenistic errors of P. Quesnel, numbers 79-85 (*DS* 2479-2485); PIUS VII, Letter *Magno et acerbo* (3 September 1816) on the versions of sacred Scripture (*DS* 2710-2712). On this long, disturbing chapter in the history of the Catholic Church, C.M. MARTINI does not neglect to speak in S. LYONNET and others (eds.), *La Bibbia nella Chiesa dopo la "Dei Verbum"*, Rome: Ediz. Paoline, 1969, pp. 161-169; however, the *Enchiridion Biblicum*, which we are using, does fail to document this, as it would have been appropriate for it to do and legitimate for us to expect.

[193] For the rights of Christian faithful *vis-à-vis* catechists, see VATICAN II, *DV*, § 25 (*EB* 705); *vis-à-vis* biblical scholars and theologians, see *DV* § 23 (*EB* 703); *vis-à-vis* bishops, see *DV* § 25 (*EB* 706). The CIC, can. 213, lays down *per modum unius*: "Ius est christifidelibus ut ex spiritualibus Ecclesiae bonis, praesertim ex verbo Dei et sacramentis, adiumenta a sacris Pastoribus accipiant". Of their most fundamental rights in relation to sacred Scripture, namely those as depositaries, custodians, interpreters and witnesses, the CIC makes no mention. It would have been good to do so, given the grave abuses of the past. It seems that CIC, can. 825, still retains some trace of these. Its restrictions on the printing and translation of sacred Scripture recall those of the Code of Benedict XV (1917), cann. 1385 § 1, 1° and 1391, and these, in turn, recall those of the normative of the Counter-Reformation. One could have expected an improvement after Vatican Council II, especially after *DV* (see, in particular, the sentences, significantly generic, with which §§ 22 and 25 touch upon the subject).

(c) *"Vulgate" biblical interpretation.* The preachers and the catechists of the Church, as evangelizers (as well as recipients and depositaries-witnesses) of the Bible, endowed with their own particular charisma for the exercise of this ministry and bound to assume the sacred Scripture as substance and rule of their teaching[194], have the ability and the duty to "interpret" the sacred books, in the sense that they can and must devote themselves to teaching and expounding the biblical Word[195]. They also have the right (*vis-à-vis* biblical scholars, theologians and bishops), to be informed of the results of exegesis and of the hermeneutical developments regarding the Scriptures.

(d) *"Exegetical" biblical interpretation.* The Biblical scholars of the Church, as experts in the exegesis (exegetes, as well as recipients and depositaries-witnesses) of the Bible, endowed with their own particular charisma to research and expound the original sense (or the original senses)[196] of the biblical Word and charged with exercising it for the benefit of all[197], have the capacity and the duty to "interpret" the sacred books, and namely to apply themselves with zeal, accuracy[198] and ecclesial responsibility in establishing the probable authentic text (or its probable history), in determining the probable genuine meaning of the Scripture (or its probable history), in clarifying not only what is said but also why it is said, in distinguishing the cultural and temporal aspects in the scriptural text, in

---

[194] VATICAN II, *DV*, § 24 (*EB* 704) and § 25 (*EB* 705): each "minister of the Word" "verbi divini amplissimas divitias… cum fidelibus sibi commissis communicare debet"; *DV* § 21 (*EB* 701): "omnis… praedicatio ecclesiastica… sacra Scriptura nutriatur et regatur oportet".

[195] VATICAN II, *DV* § 25 (*EB* 705): for the exercise of the "ministry of the Word" "assidua lectione sacra atque exquisito studio in Scripturis haerere necesse est". This study has to include a knowledge of the original sense and of the actualised sense, because preachers and catechists must propose the actualised Word of God and account for the actualization with which they re-propose the biblical Word.

[196] The original sense, or the original senses, those gradually assumed over the process of drafting of the text until its final version. In fact, it is not infrequent to find biblical passages which are the result of various phases of sedimentation; likewise there are biblical passages that take on new meaning from their transposition into contexts differing from their original one.

[197] Cf. 1Cor 12. This gift comes from God. The ecclesiastical authorities have to recognise this gift, taking care not to extinguish it.

[198] I mean: by observing the requirements and the criteria set by Scripture in the matter of exegetical interpretation, and by making use of all the techniques of the historical-exegetical sciences.

highlighting the probable divine pedagogy, and in presenting the results of their research to theologians and bishops, aware that their specialist (exegetical) interpretation must be completed with the specialist (hermeneutical) interpretation of the hermeneuts[199]. They have at the same time the right (*vis-à-vis* the theologians and the bishops), to be encouraged to investigate those biblical teachings which seem to be inadequate within the cultural contexts and historical circumstances of the contemporary world, and they also have the right (*vis-à-vis* the bishops) and the duty to exercise in freedom both their ministry as scholars and their ministry as expounders of the results of their own research[200].

(e) *"Hermeneutic-propounding" biblical interpretation.* The theologians of the Church, as experts in hermeneia (hermeneuts as well as recipients and depositaries-witnesses) of the Bible, endowed with their own particular charisma to elaborate and propound an actualized sense (or actualized senses) of the biblical Word, and charged with exercising this charisma for the advantage of all[201], have the capacity and the duty to "interpret" the sacred books, that is to say to familiarize themselves with the results of the exegetes and to apply themselves with zeal, correctness[202] and ecclesial responsibility in taking care to "disincarnate" the divine Word from the cultural and historical conditioning of the early scriptural expressions, to try to "re-incarnate" it faithfully in contemporary cultures and historical realities and to communicate the results of their work of actualization to the bishops for their supervision, aware that their own specialized (propositive hermeneutics, unofficial yet authoritative) interpretation has to be examined and confirmed by the specialized (adjudicative hermeneutics, official) interpretation of the hermeneuts-judges. They have at the same time the right (*vis-à-vis* the biblical scholars) and the duty to be informed of the results of exegetical studies, as well as the right (*vis-à-vis* the bish-

---

[199] Otherwise one falls into "fundamentalism", condemned, in particular, by the PONTIFICAL BIBLICAL COMMISSION, *IntB*, I, F and "Conclusion" (*EB* 1381-1390 and 1567) or into "biblicism", condemned, in particular, by JOHN PAUL II, Encyclical *Letter Fides et Ratio* (14 September 1998), § 55; *quoad rem* already in *Dtc* § 11 (*EB* 1252).

[200] Cf. below, fn. 232.

[201] What was written above with respect to biblical scholars (fn. 197) applies to theologians as well.

[202] I mean: by observing the requirements and the criteria which Scripture sets for hermeneutical interpretation, and by making use of all the techniques of the hermeneutical arts.

ops) and the duty to freely exercise both their ministry as scholars and their ministry as expounders of the results of their studies[203].

(f) *"Hermeneutical-judicial" biblical interpretation.* The bishops, as judges of the ecclesial hermeneia (interpreters of the last instance as well as recipients and depositaries-witnesses)[204] of the Bible, and endowed with their own special charisma to keep the Word of God intact and alive and by virtue of the apostolic mandate conferred on them[205], have the capacity and the duty to "interpret" the sacred books, that is, to take note of the results obtained by biblical scholars regarding the original sense of the biblical Word, to examine and judge, in harmony with the *sensus fidei* of the people of God, the proposals of theologians regarding the actualized sense of the biblical word, and to apply themselves with zeal, correctness[206] and ecclesial responsibility to guaranteeing the correct development of the tradition. At the same time, they have the right (and the duty) to promote and coordinate the exercise of the various functions of the ministry of the Word while respecting the charisms and responsibilities of each; in particular, they must work to propagate the sacred books and disseminate the knowledge of them throughout the world, to promote the devoted, assiduous and regular reading of the sacred Scriptures by the Christian faithful, to guide the dissemination of the faith by the preachers and catechists, to encourage the scientific research of the biblical scholars and to promote the doctrinal advances of the theologians.

Having completed this summary overview of the individual forms of biblical interpretation, the last of these remains to be examined in greater detail. While the other two forms of qualified interpretation (those of the biblical scholars and of the theologians) have already been discussed at length, the interpretation of the bishops – which is decisive – has only been marginally considered to this point. It now needs to be further clarified and justified[207].

---

[203] What applies to biblical scholars, applies also to theologians. See below, fn. 232.

[204] For the necessary clarifications, see below.

[205] VATICAN II, *DV* § 8 (*EB* 680) speaks of "qui cum episcopatus successione charisma veritatis certum acceperunt".

[206] I mean: proving to be true *servants* of the divine word, and not its *masters*. Cf. what follows.

[207] The analysis that follows seeks to highlight the presence of some theoretical ambiguities, that may give rise to practical distortions, and strives to propose a solution to these,

The Catholic statute of biblical interpretation recognizes that the bishops have a special and exclusive role. It is necessary to properly understand the nature of this role, its methods and its limits, otherwise there is a concrete risk of involutions on a theoretical level and abuses on a practical level.

1. (*"Interpretatio authentica", "iudicium ultimum"*). In its Dogmatic Constitution on Divine Revelation, the Second Vatican Council speaks of this role of the bishops in two ways: first, by saying that the bishops give the "authentic interpretation"[208]; second, by saying that they issue a "judgment", a "final judgement" on the interpretation of the "exegetes"[209]. In support of the first affirmation, reference is made to an Encyclical Letter of Pius XII[210]; in support of the second, the reference is to the Dogmatic Constitution on the Catholic Faith of the First Vatican Council, which reiterated a parenthetical statement present in the Decree on the Interpretation of Scripture of the Council of Trent: "…sancta mater Ecclesia [= the *hierarchy* of the Church], cuius est iudicare de vero sensu et interpretatione Scripturarum Sanctarum"[211]. As emerges from these references,

---

enhancing and extending the doctrine (letter and spirit) that the hierarchical magisterium has been enunciating in this last century [the XXth century, *ed.*], especially in the solemn conciliar texts.

[208] Vatican II, *DV* § 10 (*EB* 684): quoted above, in fn. 57. See also the way in which the Reporter expresses himself in presenting the text of § 10 to the conciliar Fathers in the course of its drafting (the passages are found above, in fn. 53, and below, in fn. 218). Cf. Pontifical Biblical Commission, *IntB*, III, B, 3 (*EB* 1472).

[209] Vatican II, *DV* § 12 (*EB* 690): "Exegetae autem est secundum has regulas adlaborare ad sacrae Scripturae sensum penitius intelligendum et exponendum, ut quasi praeparato studio, iudicium Ecclesiae maturetur. Cuncta enim haec, de ratione interpretandi Scripturam, Ecclesiae iudicio ultime subsunt…". The expression "quasi praeparato studio, iudicium Ecclesiae maturetur" was taken word for word from Leo XIII, *PrD* (*EB* 109).

[210] Vatican II, *DV* § 10, note 16 (*EB* 684). The reference is to the Encyclical Letter *Humani generis* (12 August 1950), *AAS* 42, 1950, pp. 568-569 (*DS* 3886; *EB* 611): "Quod quidem depositum [= the sources of divine Revelation] nec singulis christifidelibus nec ipsis theologis divinus Redemptor concredidit authentice interpretandum, sed soli Ecclesiae Magisterio". Leo XIII, in *PrD* (18 November 1893; *EB* 109), had spoken of scriptural passages "quorum sensus authentice declaratus est, aut…, aut per Ecclesiam…", "sive solemni iudicio, sive ordinario et universali magisterio"", quoting an expression employed by Vatican I, *DF*, chap. 3 (*DS* 3011; cf. below, fn. 215).

[211] Vatican II, *DV* § 12, note 26 (*EB* 690). The passage from Vatican Counc. I is taken from *DF*, cap. II (*DS* 3007; *EB* 78). The Tridentine phrase, quoted by Vatican Counc. I, is taken from the *Decretum de vulgata editione Bibliorum et de modo interpretandi s. Scripturam* (4 February 1546), *DS* 1507 (*EB* 62); a phrase repeated also by Pius IV, *Pro-*

the traditional formulation of the specific and exclusive role of the bishops as interpreters of the Scriptures presents them as "judges" of interpretation (however, two specifications are new: they are *final* judges, and they are judges of the interpretation of the *exegetes*). In recent years, this formulation has been joined with that presenting the bishops as "*authentic* interpreters".

Now: neither of these developments in the way this role is described are felicitous.

2. (*Sub verbo Dei*). The object of the episcopal judgement is not the Word of God, but rather its interpretation (its meaning or the meaning attributed to it by the interpreters)[212]. The obligatory basis of this judgement is the written Word of God; its obligatory criterion is the substantial correspondence between the interpretation (in its hermeneutical outcome; cf. below, point 6) and the written Word of God[213]. "Magisterium [= the hierarchical *magisterium*] non supra Verbum Dei est, sed eidem ministrat, docens nonnisi quod traditum est, quatenus illud ex divino mandato et Spiritu Sancto assistente, pie audit, sancte custodit et fideliter exponit, ac ea omnia ex hoc uno fidei deposito haurit

---

fessio Tridentina (13 November 1564; *DS* 1863) and by LEO XIII, *PrD* (*EB* 108). On the significance to be afforded to the term "Ecclesia" in these two documents, I have provided clarifications above, in fn. 59.

[212] INTERNATIONAL THEOLOGICAL COMMISSION., *Ip*, C, I, 3 (*EB* 1216): "Magisterium de verbo Dei iudicium non profert, sed de rectitudine eius interpretationis".

[213] This criterion cannot be replaced by any other; not even by the "sensus, quem tenuit ac tenet sancta Mater Ecclesia", nor by the "unanimis consensus Patrum". The COUNCIL OF TRENT (*DSS-II*; *EB* 62) – taken up by VATICAN COUNC. I (*DF*, cap. II; *DS* 3007; *EB* 78), and then again by LEO XIII, *PrD* (*EB* 108); *Vig.* (*EB* 141) –, "ad coercenda petulantia ingenia", demands the observance of these two interpretative criteria. They may be valid as more proximate, more immediate, criteria for the common interpretation; not as ultimate, decisive criteria for the qualified interpretation, which has the task of dedicating itself either to seeking better knowledge of the original sense or to elaborating an actualised sense. The interpretation of the Church, even though it goes back centuries, and the interpretation of the Fathers, even if it were unanimous, are to be regarded as *norma normata* by the *norma normans*, which remains and will remain the Scripture alone. An interpretation cannot be judged to be false simply because it is innovative (cf. below, fn. 226). Thus, VATICAN II, *DV* § 12, dealing with the specialized interpretation (of biblical scholars and theologians), whose task is of "adlaborare ad sacrae Scripturae sensum penitius intelligendum et exponendum", demands only that they do it "ratione habita vivae totius Ecclesiae Traditionis". On this subject, see also the following point 3.

quae tamquam divinitus revelata credenda proponit"[214]. The episcopal magisterium's authority to define (limited to questions of faith and of morals) "tantum patet quantum divinae Revelationis patet depositum, sancte custodiendum et fideliter exponendum"[215]. The first requirement of biblical interpretation (cf. above, 2.1, a) – that of faithfulness to the written Word, supreme and inviolable Authority – must be respected by all members of the Catholic Church, and *imprimis* by its bishops[216], both when they themselves interpret, and when, exercising their office, they judge the interpretations of others. The *raison d'être* for the judgment of bishops over the interpretations of the Bible, and for their mandate to issue judgement on the matter, is to maintain the "integrity"[217] of the Word of God, to provide certainty on its meaning[218]; not to impose a meaning on the Scriptures at their discretion[219].

---

[214] Vatican II, *DV* § 10 (*EB* 684). The words "docens nonnisi quod traditum est" were introduced – according to the Report to the schema of September 1964 – "ut et fratres seiuncti statim videant magisterium in Ecclesia catholica nullatenus ut *dominum*, sed ut *ministrum* verbi Dei considerari, quippe quod suum sit illud interpretari, nihil addendo vel subtrahendo"; the words "pie audit" were introduced – according to the Report on the schema of September 1965 – "ad ulterius indicandum dependentiam Magisterii a deposito revelato atque huiusce, respectu ad illud, trascendentiam". Cf. F. Gil Hellín, *Concilii Vaticani II Synopsis. Dei Verbum*, Città del Vaticano: LEV, 1993, pp. 78 and 79.

[215] Vatican II, *LG* § 25 (*C.Vat.II - Doc.*, 346); cf. also the end of this same paragraph (*C.Vat.II - Doc.*, 347). To be believed with "divine and catholic faith" are "quae in verbo Dei scripto vel tradito continentur et ab Ecclesia sive solemni iudicio, sive ordinario et universali magisterio tamquam divinitus revelata credenda proponuntur", Vatican I, *DF*, chap. 3 (*DS* 3011).

[216] Shepherds should be models for their flock, 1 Pet 5,3. Cf. Vatican II, Decree *Christus Dominus* (28 October 1965), § 15 (*C.Vat.II - Doc.*, 607); *LG* § 25 (*C.Vat.II - Doc.*, 350); § 41 (*C.Vat.II - Doc.*, 391). In the *Decretum Gratiani* (I Pars, Distinctio 9, can. 8: "Litteris omnium episcoporum sacra scriptura preponatur") the following passage of Augustine (*De baptismo*, II, 3) is found: "Quis nesciat sanctam scripturam canonicam, tam veteris quam novi testamenti, certis terminis suis contineri, eamque posterioribus omnibus episcoporum litteris ita preponi, ut de illa omnino dubitari et disceptari non possit, utrum verum vel utrum rectum sit, quicquid in ea scriptum constiterit esse?"

[217] Vatican II, *DV* § 7 (*EB* 677-678).

[218] In the Reports presenting the scheme of *Dei Verbum* of September 1964, regarding the interpretative role of the bishops (§ 10), one reads: "Ut autem de genuino sensu Depositi revelati absoluta habeatur certitudo, necesse est ut Magisterium qua tale suam edicat sententiam. Ad illud unum enim spectat ea omnia quae hereditate divina per Apostolos Ecclesia accepit authentice interpretari, ac de eorum Traditioni apostolicae fidelitate iudicare". Cf. Gil Hellín (cit. in fn. 53), pp. 495-496.

[219] The axiom of E. Betti (*Teoria generale dell'interpretazione*, vol. I, Milano: Giuffrè,

3. (*Interpretatio "authentica"? iudicium "ultimum"?*). It therefore seems improper to present the judgment of the bishops on the sense and on the interpretations of the Bible as "authentic" interpretation of the sacred Scripture[220]. Properly speaking, it is "judicial" interpretation only. The biblical Word, "inspired" by the Spirit, is divine Word. Only God, the Author of the Scriptures, can provide authentic interpretation of them. The interpretation of the bishops (the judgement they issue on the interpretations of the biblical Word), "assisted" by the Spirit, is a human word; it does not represent a new "revelation"; it does not modify or add to the divine deposit of the faith.[221] Consequently, the claim to "irreformability", advanced by the hierarchy regarding its own doctrinal definitions (= its own interpretative judgements)[222], appears difficult to understand. By their very nature, the judicial interpretations of the bishops seem to be perpetually "reformable" by the same judicial organ which has issued them. After all, if the divine Word of the sacred Scriptures itself, inasmuch as it is embodied in truly human words,

---

1990, pp. 102, 305) – sensus non est inferendus, sed efferendus – is particularly suited to biblical interpretation, and *imprimis* to the biblical interpretation of the bishops.

[220] Cf. above, footnotes 208, 210 and 218. VATICAN II, *LG* § 25 (*C.Vat.II - Doc.*, 345) writes that the bishops are "doctores authentici seu auctoritate Christi praediti". In qualifying the biblical interpretation of the bishops as "authentic", it ought to be made clear, in line with this conciliar passage, that the intention is only to state that their judicial interpretation is "authoritative", rests on a divine mandate (cf. *DV* § 10: the magisterium of the Church "cuius auctoritas in nomine Iesu Christi exercetur"). However, the expression could still lend itself to undesirable misunderstandings.

[221] VATICAN II, *LG* § 25 (*C.Vat.II - Doc.*, 346): "Cum autem Romanus Pontifex sive Corpus Episcoporum cum eo sententiam definiunt, eam proferunt secundum Revelationem, cui omnes stare et conformari tenentur et quae... in Ecclesia sancte servatur et fideliter exponitur...; novam vero revelationem publicam tamquam ad divinum fidei depositum pertinentem non accipiunt".

The bishops can give "authentic" interpretation of the documents they themselves issue: for example, of conciliar decrees (cf. the work of the PONT. COMM. DECRETIS CONCILII VATICANI II INTERPRETANDIS), of the laws of the Church (cf. JOHN PAUL II, Apostolic Constitution *Pastor Bonus*, 28 June 1988, artt. 154-158).

[222] VATICAN II, *LG* § 25 (*C.Vat.II - Doc.*, 346): when the Roman Pontiff, "ut universalis Ecclesiae magister supremus" [poor choice of words! Cf. Mt 23,10], "doctrinam de fide vel moribus definitivo actu proclamat", his definitions "ex sese, et non ex consensu Ecclesiae, irreformabiles merito dicuntur, quippe quae sub assistentia Spiritus Sancti... prolatae sint..., nec ulla ad aliud iudicium appellationem patiantur". Cf. INTERNATIONAL THEOLOGICAL COMMISSION., *Ip*, C, I, 3 (*EB* 1216): "Tempus posterius [to the judgement issued by the hierarchical magisterium on the correctness of a biblical interpretation] nullum potest regredi ultra id quod iam in dogmate sub Spiritu Sancti assistentia tamquam clavis pro Scriptura legenda formam accepit".

is subject to historicity and reformability – as is well known to biblical scholars, but also, in some measure, to those who have studied the Bible a little
– and thus requires continuous actualization, it is hard to understand how the
human word, however authoritative, found in the judicial interpretations of
the bishops could be presumed to be, by contrast, free from such historicity
and reformability, immune from the need for continuous actualization[223]. As
such, even the qualification of the interpretative judgement of the bishops
as "final" appears to be rather ambiguous, and thus requires further clarification. It seems that this judgement can be called "final" in the sense that it
is to be issued only at the conclusion of a frank and thorough consultation
of experts and the entire ecclesial community (cf. the following points 4-7);
but can it also be called "final" in the sense of "definitive"[224]? *Si sub verbo*

---

[223] In practice, when it is necessary to remedy doctrines that have by now become
wholly indefensible, the hierarchical magisterium felicitously shows that it is able to forget
its theory of the "irreformability" of its doctrines. For a recent example, see my essay
"Magi-stero pontificio e sacra Scrittura (due pagine di storia)", *Anthropotes* 8 (1992) 239-
272 (reprinted with some additions in the collection *Economia di mercato e cristianesimo*,
cit. in fn. 95 above, pp. 111-169); [and in A. TOSATO, *Vangelo e ricchezza, nuove prospettive
esegetiche*, cit. in fn. 113 above, pp. 125-186, *ed.*]; and the considerations in *Anthropotes*
13 (1997) 172. For other, well-known cases, see J.T. NOONAN, *jr.*, "Development in Moral
Doctrine", *Theological Studies* 54 (1993) 662-677 p.

If this is so *de jure* and *de facto*, then, when the bishops have issued a judicial interpretation on questions touching upon the constitution and mission of the Church and concerning
all its members (as, for example, in the recent case of the ordination of women to priest-
hood), does this remove the duty/right of the specialists to investigate (cf. below, fn. 232)
and of the community of believers to debate (cf. below, fn. 244) the matter, provided that
obedience and respect for the hierarchical decision are guaranteed?

[224] This seems to be the current official doctrine of the Catholic hierarchical magisterium. In fact, it distinguishes among: (1) truths contained in the Niceo-Costantinopo-
litan symbol of faith; (2) truths that the hierarchical magisterium proposes for belief as
divinely revealed; (3) *truths proposed by the Church in a definitive way*; (4) teachings
that the hierarchical magisterium proposes, but without the intention of proclaiming them
by a definitive act; cf. the *Professio fidei* (9 January 1989) of the CONGREGATION FOR THE
DOCTRINE OF THE FAITH (*AAS* 81, 1989, 104-106). In the *Nota doctrinalis Professionis fidei
formulam extremam enucleans* (29 June 1998; *L'Osservatore Romano* 30 June-1 July 1998,
pp. 4-5), the same CONGREGATION explains, with regard to the third category, that these
are doctrines that the hierarchical magisterium has not proposed as formally revealed, but
that it has either defined or taught as "sententia definitive tenenda" (for this formula, see
VATICAN II, *LG* § 25). As an illustration we recall, among others, the doctrine on priestly
ordination to be reserved only to men, with a double reference: to JOHN PAUL II, Apostolic
Letter *Ordinatio sacerdotalis* (22 May 1994; *AAS* 86, 1994, 548), § 4, where it is declared
"Ecclesiam facultatem nullatenus habere ordinationem sacerdotalem mulieribus confer-
endi, *hancque sententiam ab omnibus Ecclesiae fidelibus esse definitive tenendam* " (my

Dei, ergo semper sub iudice[225]. Once it has been duly made and issued, the hierarchical judgement must be obediently followed by all the faithful (not supinely, because there could be a contrary imperative of conscience, and then *oboedire oportet Deo magis quam hominibus*). However, new exegetical data, as well as new hermeneutical demands, can always come to light (or, likewise, it can happen that the judges-interpreters may reconsider the effective, continuing validity of the grounds that had determined their decision), and as such oblige the judging hierarchy to reconsider its previous judgment and to "reform" it"[226].

---

italics); and to the CONGREGATION FOR THE DOCTRINE OF THE FAITH, *Responsum ad dubium circa doctrinam in Epist. ap. "Ordinatio sacerdotalis" traditam* (28 October 1995; *AAS* 87, 1995, 1114), where the response is "Affirmative" to the doubt raised "utrum doctrina, tradita tamquam definitive tenenda in Epis. Ap. "Ordinatio sacerdotalis"..., ut pertinens *ad fidei depositum* intelligenda sit". In this last document, one reads that "praesentibus adiunctis, Romanus Pontifex... eandem doctrinam per formalem declarationem tradidit, explicite enuntians quod semper, quod ubique et quod ab omnibus tenendum est, utpote ad fidei depositum pertinens".

On this question, one may see the recent article of Ch. THEOBALD, "Le discours 'définitif' du magistère. Pourquoi avoir peur d'une réception créatrice?", *Concilium* (French ed.) 279, 1999, 85-95.

[225] The word of God stands over even the judgements of the hierarchical magisterium, cutting "more than a double-edged sword", penetrating "to the point of division of soul and spirit, joints and marrow" and discerning the "feelings and the thoughts of the heart; before Him no creature can hide, but all is naked and exposed in his eyes and to Him we must account" (*Heb* 4,12-13). This is a datum of faith and also of historical experience.

[226] Sadly known are the judgements promulgated by the HOLY OFFICE and the PONTIFICAL BIBLICAL COMMISSION on the subject of exegesis (*EB* 135-136; 160; 161; 181-184; 187-189; 276-280; 324-331; 332-339; 383-389; 390-398; 399-400; 401-406; 407-410; 411-413; 414-416; 513-514; 515-519); on the said Commission, cf. below, fn. 234. In the *Lettre au Card. Suhard* (16 January 1948; *AAS* 40, 1948, 45-48; *EB* 577-581), the PONTIFICAL BIBLICAL COMMISSION itself "concedes" that some of its previous decrees, promulgated in response to exegetical questions (on the historicity of the accounts contained in the "historical books" of the Bible, on the Mosaic authorship of the Pentateuch, and on the historical character of the first three chapters of Genesis), "ne s'opposent nullement à un examen ultérieur vraiment scientifique de ces problèmes d'après les résultats acquis pendant ces quarante dernières années"; and citing *DaS* (*EB* 564) it recalls that the Catholic exegete must, among other things, seek "de satisfaire pleinement aux conclusions certaines des sciences profanes" and that "the sons of the Church" must "se garder de ce zèle tout autre que prudent, qui estime devoir attaquer ou tenir en suspicion tout ce qui est nouveau" (*EB* 578-579). The great advances in biblical sciences, their importance for reaching a better understanding of sacred Scripture, and the need to pursue them with alacrity were recalled with particular emphasis by PIUS XII in *DaS* (see, for example, *EB* 546 and 555).

4. (*Per media apta*). In issuing their judicial interpretations, the bishops are bound – in accordance with the Dogmatic Constitution on the
Church of Vatican Council II – to duly investigate and give apt expression to the sacred Scriptures, taking care, as is their official duty and in
proportion to the importance of the case, to make use of adequate aids[227].
Let us translate the rather abstract and generic language of the council
into more concrete and specific terms. The bishops, in their interpretative
judgement, must comply not only with the fundamental requirement for
the Catholic interpretation of the Bible (faithfulness to the written Word
of God), but also with the connected principle (faithfulness to the Word
of God written in truly human words), thus carrying out an interpretative
process that embraces exegesis (= "duly investigate") and hermeneia
(= "suitably express") (cf. above, 2.1), and completing this in accordance
with the biblical criteria of interpretation (those for exegesis and those
for hermeneia; cf. above, 2.2). However, in order to perform exegesis and
hermeneia according to the biblical criteria and in a manner appropriate to
the present times (which require an ever higher degree of specialization
in every branch of knowledge), today more than ever it is necessary for
them to turn to the help of specialists, experts in these disciplines. For
their "judicial" interpretation, the bishops cannot exempt themselves from
making use of the "specialist" ("prudential") interpretation of exegetes and
hermeneuts of true profession[228].

5. (*Diairèseis charismàtōn*). Further clarification is necessary here. The
recourse to interpreters-exegetes and interpreters-hermeneuts (the experts
in exegesis and hermeneia) by the bishops in order to ensure the correct
exercise of their office as judges-interpreters, is not so much a question of
opportuness or of necessity dictated by modern times, as it is a question
of obedience to a divine imperative derived from the constitutive real-

---

[227] VATICAN II, *LG* § 25 (*C.Vat.II - Doc.*, 347): "Cum autem sive Romanus Pontifex sive
Corpus Episcoporum cum eo sententiam definiunt, eam proferunt secundum ipsam Revelationem... Ad quam rite indagandam et apte enuntiandam, Romanus Pontifex et Episcopi,
pro officio suo et rei gravitate, per media apta, sedulo operam navant". Cf. INTERNATIONAL
THEOLOGICAL COMMISSION, *Ip*, C, I, 3 (*EB* 1216).
[228] I say "of true profession", meaning whereby to exclude "palace", "court" exegetes
and hermeneuts. In our case, in fact, this is not a formality, such that it can be done away
with in private, through some sort of bargain. Such courtiers should not be counted among
these *media apta*.

ity of the Church and expressed clearly in the sacred Scripture. "There are diversities of charismas (διαιρέσεις χαρισμάτων), but one only is the Spirit; there are are diversities of ministries (διαιρέσεις διακονιῶν), but one only is the Lord; there are diversities of works (διαιρέσεις ἐνεργημάτων), but one only is the Lord, who accomplishes all in all. And to each person is given the manifestation of the Spirit for the common good (ἑκάστῳ δὲ δίδοται ἡ φανέρωσις τοῦ πνεύματος πρὸς τὸ συμφέρον)... all these things are operated by one and the same Spirit who distributes them to each as He wills (διαιροῦν ἰδίᾳ ἑκάστῳ καθὼς βούλεται)... The eye cannot say to the hand: I have no need of you (Χρείαν σου οὐκ ἔχω); nor the head to the feet: I have no need of you (Χρείαν ὑμῶν οὐκ ἔχω)[229]. The last Council [Vatican II, *ed.*] returned several times to this scriptural teaching, which is both of faith and of morals, recalling it with particular insistence in various documents, as if to urge more faithful observance of it[230]. It is, therefore, by explicit divine will that the bishops, in exercising their hierarchical magisterium, must recognize[231], respect, value and appropriately use the

---

[229] 1Cor 12,4-30. Paul repeats an analogous teaching in Rom 12,3-9: since, by divinely bestowed grace, distinct charismas are possessed in the Church (ἔχοντες δὲ χαρίσματα κατὰ τὴν χάριν τὴν δοθεῖσαν ἡμῖν διάφορα), all must strive to best practise the charisma they have received. None is allowed to think more highly of themselves than they ought (μὴ ὑπερφρονεῖν παρ᾽ ὃ δεῖ φρονεῖν). To each, God has distributed his portion of faith (ἑκάστῳ ὡς ὁ θεὸς ἐμέρισεν μέτρον πίστεως), that is, He has assigned to each his place and his function in the community of believers with his specific charisma so that he may contribute his specific service (τὸ...καθ᾽ εἷς ἀλλήλων μέλη) to all other members. In 1Pet 4,10, one reads: "let each (ἕκαστος), according to the charisma received (καθὼς ἔλαβεν χάρισμα), put it at the service of the others (εἰς ἑαυτοὺς αὐτὸ διακονοῦντες), as good administrators of the manifold grace of God (ὡς καλοὶ οἰκονόμοι ποικίλης χάριτος θεοῦ)". See also Eph 4,1.

[230] Vatican II, *LG* §§ 12, 18, 30 and 35 (*C.Vat.II - Doc.*, 317, 328, 361 and 374); Decree *Apostolicam Actuositatem* (18 November 1965), §§ 3 and 30 (*C.Vat.II - Doc.*, 921 and 1030); Decree *Ad Gentes* (7 December 1965), §§ 23 and 28 (*C.Vat.II - Doc.*, 1171 and 1189); Decree *Presbyterorum Ordinis* (7 December 1965), § 9 (*C.Vat.II - Doc.*, 1272).

[231] "Recognising" implies discernment (δοκιμάζειν), cf. 1Jn 4,1 (in truth, the discerning here concerns the authenticity of the prophetic discourses of those who are "charismatics" *par excellence*: μὴ παντὶ πνεύματι πιστεύετε, ἀλλὰ δοκιμάζετε τὰ πνεύματα εἰ ἐκ τοῦ θεοῦ ἐστιν, ὅτι πολλοὶ ψευδοπροφῆται ἐξεληλύθασιν εἰς τὸν κόσμον). A specific charisma is conferred for the exercise of such a task, cf. 1Cor 12,10 (here too the "discernment" is referred to "prophecy": ἄλλῳ διακρίσεις πνευμάτων). Therefore, it is to be exercised in the Spirit, for the Spirit and for the common benefit of the Church, taking good care not to grieve the Spirit (Eph 4,30), not to extinguish it (1Thess 5,19-21: τὸ πνεῦμα μὴ σβέννυτε, προφητείας μὴ ἐξουθενεῖτε· πάντα δὲ δοκιμάζετε, τὸ καλὸν κατέχετε), not to blaspheme Him (Mk 3,28-30 and parallels; *Gospel of Thomas*, 44).

specialized magisterium of exegetes and hermeneuts; and it is likewise by explicit divine will that the exegetes and hermeneuts, in exercising their specialized magisterium, must lay claim to those areas under their domain and the freedoms, be they scientific or sapiential, which not the bishops, but God has entrusted to their responsibility[232].

6. (*Iudicium de exegesi?*). To date, in the Church, clear light has yet to be shed on the fundamental phenomenological, conceptual and terminological distinction relating to interpretation (relating, specifically, to the interpretation of ancient texts that are expected to be normative for the present and, accordingly, also to the interpretation of the Bible). A formal distinction between *exegesis* and *hermeneia* as intrinsically different and necessarily complementary steps of a single interpretative process has not been established[233]. However, once the congruence of and need for such a distinction is accepted, and the distinction is adopted, then it is no longer enough to say, generically, that the role of the bishops is that of judging biblical "interpretation". It is necessary to specify whether their judicial task concerns both sides of interpretation, the exegetical and the hermeneutical, or only one of these, and, in that case, which of the two. Now, given the fact that exegesis aims at ascertaining scientifically the genuine letter and original sense of the biblical text, as well as to communicate the results of

---

[232] Even without referring to the theological foundation of being in Christ and the distribution of charisms, VATICAN II, *GS* § 62 (*C.Vat.II - Doc.*, 1532) advises: "Ut vero munus suum exercere valeant, agnoscatur fidelibus, sive clericis sive laicis, iusta libertas inquirendi, cogitandi necnon mentem suam in humilitate et fortitudine aperiendi in iis in quibus peritia gaudent". Cf. *LG* §§ 18 e 37 (*C.Vat.II - Doc.*, 328 and 382-385); Declaration *Gravissimum educationis* [= *GE*] (28 October 1965), § 10 (*C.Vat.II - Doc.*, 843); and also the *Lettre au Card. Suhard* of the PONTIFICAL BIBLICAL COMMISSION (*EB* 578), mentioned above in fn. 226. The new CIC has taken up this conciliar recommendation: both in can. 212, § 3: "Pro scientia, competentia et praestantia quibus pollent, ipsis [= Christifidelibus] ius est, immo et aliquando officium, ut sententiam suam de his quae ad bonum Ecclesiae pertinent sacris Pastoribus manifestent eamque, salva fidei morumque integritate ac reverentia erga Pastores, attentisque communi utilitate et personarum dignitate, ceteris christifidelibus notam faciant"; and in can. 218: "Qui disciplinis sacris incumbunt iusta libertate fruuntur inquirendi necnon mentem suam prudenter in iis aperiendi, in quibus peritia gaudent, servato debito erga Ecclesiae magisterium obsequio". See also JOHN PAUL II, *CCC* § 907. It will always be useful to refer, beyond these valuable teachings in the recent hierarchical magisterium, to the Apostle's denunciation of the false brothers who infiltrate themselves κατασκοπῆσαι τὴν ἐλευθερίαν ἡμῶν ἣν ἔχομεν ἐν Χριστῷ Ἰησοῦ, ἵνα ἡμᾶς καταδουλώσουσιν - "to spy on the freedom we have in Christ Jesus, with the aim of making us slaves" (Gal 2,4).

[233] Cf. above, 2.4 and in 2.5, fn. 141 and 142.

the scientific investigation carried out in this regard, it does not seem that this should be submitted, nor could it be submitted, to the judgement of the bishops[234]. The interpretative results of the exegetes, which are always partial and provisional, open to fine-tuning and correction, are not expressions of faith, but the fruit of science; by their very nature, they are subject to the judgement of specialists, made on the basis of scientific critique, not to hierarchical judgement, made on the basis of episcopal authority. It would be another matter if, going beyond the scope of their competence, exegetes abusively claimed that their own exegetical results had hermeneutical validity (of the Word of God for today)[235]. Exegesis is, in relation to hermeneia, a necessary study, but one that is merely preparatory, not sufficient[236]. The interpretation of the biblical Word of God also requires

---

[234] The highest levels of the Catholic hierarchy seem to have become (or to be about to become) aware of this state of affairs. This is suggested, in particular, by the law reforming the Pontifical Biblical Commission, promulgated by PAUL VI with the Motu proprio *Sedula cura* (27 June 1971; *AAS* 63, 1971, 665-669; *EB* 722-739). The Commission was established by LEO XIII with the Apostolic Letter *Vigilantiae* (30 October 1902; *AAS* 35, 1902-1903, 234-238; *EB* 137-148) as a magisterial organ of the hierarchy (composed of Cardinals and based on the model of the Pontifical Dicasteries, associated to the Congregation for the Holy Office) to judge questions of biblical interpretation with declaratory judgments (issued following approval by, and upon the order of, the Pope); the binding doctrinal character of its pronouncements was made clear, first by PIUS X, with the Motu proprio *Praestantia Scripturae* (18 November 1907; *AAS* 40, 1907, 723-726) and then again by PIUS XI on the occasion of a "responsum" of condemnation decreed by the Commission (27 February 1907; *AAS* 26, 1934, 130-131; *EB* 515-519); see also the PONTIFICAL BIBLICAL COMMISSION's Declaration *Quum de expressa* (15 February 1909; *AAS* 1, 1909, 241; *EB* 281). With the post-conciliar reform of Paul VI, the Commission was transformed into a purely consultative body (made up of biblical scholars though presided over by the Cardinal Prefect of the Congregation for the Doctrine of the Faith, formerly the Holy Office), with the task of helping the hierarchical magisterium of the Church "in sacra Scriptura interpretanda" through their studies. Exegesis here seems to be demanded to exegetes. On this significant reform, detailed and clarifying is the article of A. VANHOYE (present Secretary of the Commission [1999, ed.]), "Passé et présent de la Commission Biblique", *Gregorianum* 74 (1993) 261-275.

One may think that there are experts in exegesis among the bishops and that they, at least, are able to judge the work of other specialists in exegesis like them. But, in such cases, they would be issuing a judgement as exegetes and not as bishops, and their judgement would have weight on account of the scientific arguments adduced, not on account of the hierarchical authority of which they are invested.

[235] They would fall into the error of "fundamentalism" or "biblicism", mentioned above, in fn. 199.

[236] LEO XIII, *PrD* (*EB* 109) and VATICAN II, *DV* § 12 (*EB* 690) speak of exegetical studies as "preparatory studies" ("praeparato studio"), cf. above, fn. 209, and also INTERNATIONAL THEOLOGICAL COMMISSION, *Ip*, C, I, 3 (*EB* 1216). This seems correct, provided that

the actualization of the original meaning, a task for which, others, the hermeneuts, are competent. It seems that the exercise of judicial authority by
the bishops, who have the responsibility of maintaining the Word of God
intact and living, should regard this second, decisive side of interpretation,
in which the Word of God is elaborated for today, and this alone.

7. (*In et cum Ecclesia*). The bishops are not only bound to avail themselves of the contribution of specialists in exegesis and hermeneia for their
interpretative judgement; they are also bound to involve the entire community of believers[237]. They must decide the "sensu [fidei] quoque fidelium
subordinate concurrente"[238]. Even the Roman Pontiff, in the exercise of

---

their "preparatory" character is put in direct relation to hermeneutical elaboration, and only
indirectly, that is, through these, to the episcopal judgement.

[237] I limit myself here to discussing the necessary involvement of all Christians
(non-Catholics, therefore, included: cf. VATICAN II, *UR* § 21, *EB* 660; *DV* § 22, *EB* 702).
However, I do not disregard, nor must it be disregarded, that this involvement must be even
broader, universal; not only because it is opportune, but for reasons of a theological nature
(cf. above, 2.3, a).

[238] These words are found in the Conciliar Schema on the Revelation of February-March
1963, at the end of § 10. They were omitted in the subsequent Scheme of 1964, not because
they were disapproved but because – the Reporter explained – "*inutilia* [original italics]
redduntur post additam primam periodum [cf. above, fn. 53], ubi, cum affirmetur depositum
revelatum toti Ecclesiae esse commissum, eo ipso de momento sensus fidelium ex professo
dicitur; cui praeterea integra dedicatur paragraphus in Schemate *De Ecclesia*, n. 12 [= *LG*
§ 12]"; cf. GIL HELLÍN (cit. in fn. 53), p. 80. In illustrating this addition, introduced at the
beginning of § 10 (the entrusting of the revealed deposit *to the whole Church,* not just to the
hierarchical magisterium), the Reporter writes: "Cum Depositum revelatum donum sit divinum toti Ecclesiae factum, toti Ecclesiae consequenter officium incumbit illud conservandi,
eidem inhaerendi, idemque cunctis generationibus transmittendi. Exinde provenit quod hoc
Depositum, sicut Ecclesiae vitam regit et portat, ita a vita Ecclesiae portatur de eaque pror-
sus participat: ac propterea illum dynamicum experitur processum, ratione cuius communis
fidelium sensus, exinde profluens, *criterium cognoscendae veritatis divinitus revelatae non
semel efficiatur* [my italics]... [Thus, when carrying out its specific and exclusive role,
the hierarchical magisterium *edicit sententiam, iudicat,*] etsi multitudinis fidelium convinc-
tiones non necessario repetat, cum iisdem nihilominus quodammodo coniungitur. Veritas
enim quae tamquam de fide tenenda a Magisterio definitur si iuridice ob illam definitionem
credenda imponitur, substantialiter tamen iam fidem universae Ecclesiae attigerat: propterea quod definitionem a Magisterio est consecuta. Huiusmodi auctoritativa Magisterii
interventio nihil continet sui, nisi ipsum infallibilis auctoritatis charisma. Doctrina autem
quae proponitur non solius Magisterii, sed totius Ecclesiae est propria. Et a Magisterio
uti talis agnoscitur, quatenus divinae Revelationi consentaneam declarat atque, praesidio
Spiritus Veritatis, ita declaratam definit, eidem nihil adiciens, ab eadem nihil detrahens";
cf. GIL HELLÍN (cit. in fn. 53), pp. 495-496 (the phrases omitted here are recorded above,
in fn. 218).

his office as "supreme pastor of the Church", "communione cum ceteris episcopis immo et universa Ecclesia semper est coniunctus"[239]. In fact, the sacred deposit was entrusted to the entire Church[240]. Not by chance, nor by error, nor as if it were a sealed book; but so that it may live from it and be a witness of the Living One to the world[241]. Not only the bishops but each and every member has been endowed by God with the Spirit, and, through the Spirit, with a supernatural sense of faith and with a guide to the truth[242]. Moreover, no one in the Church has been excluded from the distribution of charismas; all have been given a particular manifestation of the Spirit, for the common good[243]. This makes the involvement of all

---

[239] CIC (1983), can. 333, § 2.

[240] Cf. above, 1.3 and here, in 2.3, b.

[241] The magisterial documents – for example: BENEDICT XV, *SpP* (*EB* 491); PIUS XII, *DaS* (*EB* 568); VATICAN II, *DV* § 25 (*EB* 705); JOHN PAUL II, *CCC* § 133 – frequently quote a passage of JEROME (*Commentarii in Isaiam Prophetam*, Prol.; PL 24, 17A; CCL 73, 1): "Si enim iuxta Apostolum Paulum (1Cor 1,24) Christus Dei virtus est, Deique sapientia, et qui nescit Scripturas, nescit Dei virtutem eiusque sapientiam. Ignoratio enim Scripturarum, ignoratio Christi est".

[242] Cf. above, 2.3, b.– VATICAN II, *LG* § 12 (*C.Vat.II - Doc.*, 316) writes: "Populus Dei sanctus de munere quoque prophetico Christi participat, vivum Eius testimonium maxime per vitam fidei ac caritatis diffundendo... Universitas fidelium, qui unctionem habent a Sancto (cf. 1Io. 2,20 et 27), in credendo falli nequit, atque hanc suam peculiarem proprietatem mediante supernaturali sensu fidei totius populi manifestat, cum "ab Episcopis usque ad extremos laicos fideles" [AUGUSTINE, *De Praedestinatione Sanctorum* 14, 27; PL 44, 980] universalem suum consensum de rebus fidei et morum exhibet. Illo enim sensu fidei, qui a Spiritu veritatis excitatur et sustentatur, Populus Dei sub ductu magisterii, ... semel traditae santis fidei (cf. Jud. 3), indefectibiliter adhaeret, recto iudicio in eam profundius penetrat eamque in vita plenius applicat". Cf. also INTERNATIONAL THEOLOGICAL COMMISSION, *Ip*, C, I, 3 (*EB* 1215): "Testimonii Iesu interpretatio indissolubiliter connexa est activitati Spiritus eius in eius testium continuitate (*apostolica successio*) atque in sensu fidei populi Dei".

[243] Cf. above, point 5 (*Diairèseis charismàton*). In the light of the fundamental biblical texts recalled in fn. 229, some of the strong warnings found in the NT are again pertinent. For example; 1Pt 5,2-3 (ποιμάνατε... μηδ' ὡς κατακυριεύοντες "pascete,... senza tiranneggiare"); Mt 20,25-28 and 23,10-12 (οἱ ἄρχοντες τῶν ἐθνῶν κατακυριεύουσιν αὐτῶν καὶ οἱ μεγάλοι κατεξουσιάζουσιν αὐτῶν. οὐχ οὕτως ἔσται ἐν ὑμῖν..., πάντες δὲ ὑμεῖς ἀδελφοί ἐστε..., ὁ δὲ μείζων ὑμῶν ἔσται ὑμῶν διάκονος); 1Cor 1,26-29 (...τὰ μωρὰ τοῦ κόσμου ἐξελέξατο ὁ θεός, ἵνα καταισχύνῃ τοὺς σοφούς, καὶ τὰ ἀσθενῆ τοῦ κόσμου ἐξελέξατο ὁ θεός, ἵνα καταισχύνῃ τὰ ἰσχυρά, καὶ τὰ ἀγενῆ τοῦ κόσμου καὶ τὰ ἐξουθενημένα ἐξελέξατο ὁ θεός, τὰ μὴ ὄντα, ἵνα τὰ ὄντα καταργήσῃ, ...). An episode narrated in the OT, in Num 11,16-30, is also instructive. Joshua's "jealousy" was out of place in Israel; it is all the more so in the Church of Jesus Christ.

Among the many texts of VATICAN II that return to this teaching (indicated above, in

absolutely necessary, especially when it comes to deciding on the correct actualization of the Word of God in general matters or in matters for which neither the bishops, nor the biblical scholars, nor the theologians can claim to have specific competence[244].

In tackling and judicially deciding the first major interpretative question (one of hermeneia) to come before the Christian community, the apostles proceeded *in et cum Ecclesia*: "It pleased the apostles, the elders, the entire assembly... It pleased the Holy Spirit and us...[245]. This was a judgement fundamental for its content; but perhaps even more fundamental for the procedure that was followed[246].

---

fn. 230), we refer to that of *LG* § 12 (*C.Vat.II - Doc.*, 318), the continuation of the passage reported in the previous footnote: "Idem praeterea Spiritus Sanctus..., dona sua "dividens singulis prout vult" (1Cor 12,11), inter omnis ordinis fideles distribuit gratias quoque speciales, quibus illos aptos et promptos reddit ad suscipienda varia opera vel officia, pro renovatione et ampliore aedificatione Ecclesiae proficua, secundum illud "Unicuique datur manifestatio Spiritus ad utilitatem" (1Cor 12,7). Quae charismata, sive clarissima, sive etiam simpliciora et latius diffusa, cum sint necessitatibus Ecclesiae apprime accomodata et utilia, cum gratiarum actione ac consolatione accipienda sunt".

[244] Cf. what was already adduced above, in fn. 232. Also particularly significant are the appeals that VATICAN II addresses to the faithful laity who, by virtue of the "sensus christianus", must not deny the Church their indispensable contribution in facing the many, complex problems of the contemporary world. Cf., for example, *GS* §§ 52 and 62 (*C.Vat. II - Doc.*, 1485-1491 and 1526-1532).

[245] Acts 15,22: ...ἔδοξε τοῖς ἀποστόλοις καὶ τοῖς πρεσβυτέροις σὺν ὅλῃ τῇ ἐκκλησίᾳ; 15,28: ἔδοξεν γὰρ τῷ πνεύματι τῷ ἁγίῳ καὶ ἡμῖν... We considered the issue at stake above, in 2.2.

[246] The INTERNATIONAL THEOLOGICAL COMMISSION, in *Ip*, C, I, 3 (*EB* 1218), gives an appropriate reminder to biblical scholars and theologians, concerning the way in which they employ the sciences in exercising their roles as exegetes-interpreters and hermeneuts-interpreters: "Hae omnes methodi [of which they make use] solummodo permanent fructuosae, dum in fidei oboedientia adhibentur et autonomae non fiunt. Communio in Ecclesia locus permanet in quo Scripturae interpretatio tuto collocatur...". It seems that a similar reminder could also be respectfully addressed to the bishops, regarding the way they make use of their authority in exercising their role of judges-interpreters.

INDEXES

I. ABBREVIATIONS

A.A.V.V   Auctores Varii
can.   canon
cf.   compare, see
chap.   chapter
cit.   cited
ed.   editor
eds.   editors
e.g.   *exempli gratia* (for example)
fasc.   fasciculum
fn.   footnote
NT   New Testament
OT   Old Testament
tom.   tomus

Abbreviations of Periodicals, Series or Works frequently quoted

AAS   *Acta Apostolicae Sedis*
CCC   Catechism of Catholic Church
CCL   Corpus Christianorum Latinorum
CIC   Codex Iuris Canonicis
CSEL   Corpus Scriptorum Christianorum Latinorum
C. Vat-Doc   Vatican Council II Documents
D   Digesto
DS   Denzinger-Schönmetzer, *Enchiridion Symbolorum*
EB   *Enchiridion Biblicum*
GCS   Griechische Christliche Schriftsteller
PG   Patrologia Greca (ed P. Migne)
PL   Patrologia Latina (ed. P. Migne)
STh   Summa Theologiae

Journals and Series (always quoted in full)

Anthropotes
Apollinaris
The Catholic Biblical Quarterly

Concilium
Gregorianum
Subsidia Biblica
Theological Studies

Abbreviations of pontifical or conciliar documents quoted
(arranged in alphabetical order according to the Council or the Pope and the year)

Benedict XV
SpP   Encyclical Letter *Spiritus Paraclitus* (15 September 1920)

Council of Trent
DSS I   *Decretum secundum de sacris Scripturis* (8 April 1546)
DSS II   *Decretum secundum de sacris Scripturis* (8 April 1546)

John Paul II
Dtc   *De tout Coeur* (23 April 1993)
Int   *L'interprétation de la Bible dans l'Eglise* (18 November 1993)
Ip   *Interpretationis problema* (31 October 1989)

Leo XIII
PrD   Encyclical Letter, *Providentissimus Deus* (18 November 1893)
Vig   Apostolic Letter *Vigilantiae* (30 October 1902)

Pius X
Lam   Congr. S. Rom. et Univ. Inquisitionis Decree *Lamentabili* (4 July 1907)
Pasc   *Pascendi dominici gregis* (8 September 1907)

Pius XI
Encyclical Letter *Mit brennender Sorge* (13 March 1937)

Pius XII
DaS   Encyclical letter *Divino afflante Spiritu* (30 September 1943)
HG   Encyclical letter *Humani generis* (12 August 1950)

Vatican Council I (1870)
DF   Dogmatic Constitution *Dei Filius* (24 April 1870)

Vatical Council II
DV   Constitution *Dei Verbum* (18 November 1965)
GE   Declaration *Gravissimum educationis* (28 October 1965)

GS Pastoral Constitution *Gaudium et spes* (7 December 1965)
LG Dogmatic Constitution *Lumen gentium* (21 November 1964)
OT *Optatam totius* (28 October 1965)
UR Decree *Unitatis redintegratio* (21 November 1964)

II. INDEX OF SOURCES[1]

a) Biblical quotations

Old Testament

Gen (Genesis)

1,27	65
17	23 fn. 38
40	36 fn. 83
41	36 fn. 83

Ex (Exodus)

10,2	34 fn. 77
12,44	62 fn. 167
13,8	34 fn. 77
19,3-8	23 fn. 39
19,10-25	31 fn. 68
20,1	31 fn. 68
20,7	47 fn. 112
20,10-11	48 fn. 118
20,12	45 fn. 105
20,19	54 fn. 139
21,1	22 fn. 35
21,6-7.9-12	32 fn. 69
21,17	45 fn. 105
23,12	48 fn. 118
23,19	22 fn. 35
24,1-11	23 fn. 39
24,3	22 fn. 35, 23 fn. 37
24,7	22 fn. 35, 23 fn. 37
24,8	23 fn. 37
24,12	15 fn. 7, 22 fn. 33 and 34
24,27	23 fn. 37

24,28	23 fn. 37
25,16	23 fn. 38
25,16.21	23 fn. 38, 32 fn.69
25,22	23 fn. 38
26,33	23 fn. 38
31,18	15 fn. 7, 22 fn. 33, 23 fn. 38
32,15	19 fn. 22, 23 fn. 38
32,16	15 fn. 7
34,1	15 fn. 7, 22 fn. 33 and 34
34,11	34 fn. 77
34,27	23 fn. 37
34,27-28	15 fn. 7
34,28	22 fn. 34
34,33.35	53
34,29	23 fn. 38
40,20	23 fn. 38
40,21	23 fn. 38

Lev (Leviticus)

5,21-26	32 fn. 69
12,3	62 fn. 167
19,12	47 fn. 112
20,9	45 fn. 105

Num (Numbers)

11,16-17.24-30	65 fn. 176
11,16-30	85 fn. 243
11,27-29	59 fn. 155

---

[1] The index includes: a) biblical quotations, listed according to the Bible of Jerusalem; b) pseudo-ephygraphical books quotations; c) New Testament Apocrypha; d) Dead Sea Scrolls quotations, listed according to F. Garcia Martinez – G. Martone, Brescia: Paideia, 1996; e) Talmud (of Jerusalem and of Babylonia); f) Classical sources; g) Patrology (Apostolic Fathers and Fathers of the Church); h) Theological sources; i) Juridical sources.

22,18 32 fn. 71
24,13 32 fn. 71
30,3 47 fn. 112

Deut (Deuteronomy)
4,1 34 fn. 77
4,2 32 fn. 72
4,9 34 fn. 77
4,13 15 fn. 7, 22 fn. 33 and 34, 23 fn. 37
4,23 23 fn. 37
4,40 26 fn. 51, 34 fn. 77
5,1 34 fn. 77
5,12-15 48 fn. 118
5,14 48 fn. 116
5,16 45 fn. 105
5,19 22 fn. 33, 23 fn. 38
5,22 15 fn. 7, 22 fn. 33, 32 fn. 73
5,29.33 26 fn. 51
5,32-33 34 fn. 77
6,4 34 fn. 77
6,6 34 fn. 77
6,7.20-25 34 fn. 77
6,24 26 fn. 51, 34 fn. 77
9,9 23 fn. 37
9,10 15 fn. 7
9,11 23 fn. 37
9,15 23 fn. 37
10,2 23 fn. 38, 32 fn. 69
10,2.4 15 fn. 7, 22 n. 34, 23 fn. 38
10,5 32 fn. 69
10,8 23 fn. 38
11,12 34 fn. 77
12,28 34 fn. 77
13,1 32 fn. 73
13,8 34 n. 77
17,10 63 fn. 171
17,18-20 24 fn. 44
17,20 34 fn. 77
19,14 45 fn. 107
23,22 47 fn. 112
27,3 22 fn. 35
27,17 45 fn. 107
28,14 34 fn. 77
28,61 22 fn. 36
29,1-3 59 fn. 156
29,9-14 23 fn. 39
29, 1-3 59 fn. 156
29,19 22 fn. 36
29,20 22 fn. 36
30,10 22 fn. 36
30,15 26 fn. 51
31,11-13 34 fn. 77
31,18
31,24 22 fn. 35
31,26 22 fn. 36
32,15
32,21 59 fn. 155
32,47 26 fn. 51
33,3-5 21 fn. 30
33,7 34 fn. 77

Josh (Joshua)
1,7 34 fn. 77
1,7-8 24 fn. 44
1,8 22 fn. 36, 34 fn. 77
8, 31.34 22 fn. 36
23,6 22 fn. 36
24,1-27 23 fn. 39
24,26 22 fn. 36

1Sam (1 Samuel)
3,9.10 34 fn. 77

2Sam (2 Samuel)
5,1-3 21 fn. 30

1Kgs (1Kings)
8,9 23 fn. 38

2Kgs (2 Kings)
11,17b 21 fn. 30
14,6 22 fn. 36
22,8.11 22 fn. 36

III. IV. INDEX OF NAMES[2]

---

[2] This index lists the biblical characters, the rabbis, the Fathers of the Church, the theologians and the jurists, the popes and the modern scholars quoted in the monograph and in the appendix as well.

APPENDIX

Angelo Tosato, biblical scholar (biblicist)[1]

He was born in Venice on 29 December 1938. He received his first and foundational religious, civic and scientific education at home, at the school of his father, Egidio Tosato: a man of rigorous Christian principles, an eminent jurist (professor of public law at the most important Italian universities) and statist, one of the Fathers of the Italian Constitution, who held various government positions during the years of reconstruction.

Having completed his secondary school studies in Rome (Liceo Tasso, 1954-1957), he studied law at La Sapienza University in Rome (1957 - 1960), philosophy and theology at the Pontifical Gregorian University (1960, license in Philosophy; 1964, license in theology). In these years, of great importance for his intellectual formation were the courses and seminars held by Bernard Lonergan, S.J, one of the most eminent thinkers of this century [the XXth century, *ed.*]; similarly formative for his ecclesial and priestly education were the sessions of the Second Vatican Council, which he had the privilege of attending from its inauguration, together with several other seminarians, as an official "stenographer".

A priest of the diocese of Rome (1963), he exercised his ministry first as a deputy parish priest (1964-1971) and later as a spiritual assistant at the Catholic University of Rome (1972-1975). This extended pastoral activity allowed him to observe the inadequacy of the ways in which the Christian message and teaching were offered – largely through the repetition of platitudes, far removed from the language, sensibility and the issues faced by his contemporaries – and led him to feel the urgency of furthering the work of *"aggiornamento"* promoted in the Catholic Church by Pope John XXIII and approved by the Second Vatican Council. Disappointed by the ill-considered improvisations of inept progressives, and similarly embittered by the authoritarian, conservative turn of others – divergent, extreme positions that both appeared to betray the letter and the spirit of the Council – he deeply felt the need to return to the Christian sources through direct contact with the original accounts: to better understand the Christian event

---

[1] The biography that follows was written by Angelo Tosato himself, on the occasion of the publication of the book edited by Dario Antiseri, *Cattolici a difesa del mercato*, Torino SEI, 1995 and updated in 1997. A short *addendum* at the end briefly accounts for the publications after 1997.

in the authenticity of its appearance and its initial development, a prerequisite to its faithful actualization.

Encouraged by his Jesuit masters, he therefore returned to the study of biblical languages and began a research thesis on scripture (about *metanoia*, under the direction of P. Donatien Mollat, S.J.), which led to a doctorate in Theology at the Gregorian University (1972); he then enrolled in the Pontifical Biblical University, having among his professors the Fathers L. Alonso-Schökel, I. De la Potterie, M. Gilbert, S. Lyonnet, C. M. Martini, A. Vanhoye, and earned a license in biblical sciences (1975). He devoted special attention to the study of the Judaic world at the time of Jesus: therefore, to Aramaic (the language spoken in Israel at that time) and to the ancient Aramaic translations of the Jewish bible (the *Targumin*, helpful for recovering the sense in which the sacred text was understood by the Israelites at that time). Invaluable guide in these difficult studies was P. Roger Le Déaut (renowned specialist in targumic Aramaic). A prolonged sojourn in Jerusalem allowed him to perfect his knowledge of the Semitic languages and biblical places and gave him contact with archaeological discoveries (especially those of the caves of Qumran). His scriptural studies at the Biblical Institute continued until he obtained his doctorate (*summa cum laude*, with a thesis on the institution of marriage, director Le Déaut).

At the same time, he started teaching (1976): at the Lateran University, responsible for the course on History of the ancient Church; at the Gregorian University, assigned to be a guide in scriptural seminars; at the Institute for Spirituality of the Gregorian University, responsible for a course on "The disciples of Jesus". From 1985, he was a professor at the John Paul II Institute for studies on marriage and family [now John Paul II Pontifical Theological Institute for Marriage and Family Sciences, *ed.*] (initially as an adjunct professor; then, from 1988, as an associate professor; from 1990 as a full professor) and at the same time at the Pontifical Biblical Institute, charged at first with teaching biblical Aramaic, then history of the institutions of the Old Testament (focusing, in alternate years, on family, political, economic and religious institutions); starting in 1998, he also was assigned the course on Matrimonial Texts (Old Testament and Qumran). In 1981, he was included among the consultants of the Pontifical Commission "De religione iudaica" at the Secretariat for Promoting Christian Unity.

His work as a scholar and lecturer resulted in a long series of publications in the biblical field[2], works of a highly scientific character, rich in implications for Christian doctrines and institutions. Among these, several may be mentioned. The 1975 essay in *Rivista biblica italiana* on neo-testamentary *metanoia* (which challenged the interpretation then in vogue and highlighted defects in the structure of the articles of the *Theologisches Wörterbuch zum Neuen Testament*]; in 1979, the essay in *Lateranum* on the Judaic roots of Christianity (specifying the content of the "great common heritage" on which a fruitful dialogue between the two religions can be based and can develop]; in 1983, in *Studia anselmiana* n. 87 (Proceedings of the I International conference on Liturgy), the essay on the sacraments of Christian initiation (clarifying, in the light of Judaic practice, the original function of Baptism and Confirmation, and the proper relation of complementarity linking one to the other); also in 1983, in *Sangue e Antropologia biblica* (*Atti della III settimana di studio*, edited by F. Vattioni), the essay on the ancient understanding – both Judaic and Greek – of the human generative process, highlighting the dependence, partially still existing, of social institutions (e.g. those relating to the status of women) and doctrinal themes (e.g. the "original sin") on the imperfect and primitive knowledge of human reproduction held in the ancient culture that is passed down and perpetuated through the Bible; in 1992, the essay in *Anthropotes* on the method of biblical interpretation, accounting for how the Catholic Church has adopted the historical-critical method and now must put it in practice, and offering an example (the abandonment of the biblical obligation that wives be subjugated to their husbands and the endorsement of a modern obligation of spousal equality) to illustrate the enormous potential for innovation that the new method brings to theological and pastoral work.

However, the primary sphere in which his research developed was that of the history of ancient Judaic and early Christian institutions, including those relating to the family, politics and economics.

(1) As for family institutions, it is worth mentioning two books: *Il matrimonio nel giudaismo antico e nel nuovo testamento* (Rome, Città Nuova, 1976; out of print) and *Il matrimonio israelitico. Una teoria generale* (Analecta Biblica, 100; Rome, Biblical Institute Press, 1982; reprinted, Rome, GBPress, 2001) [which highlight the Judaic and later Old Testament roots of the institution of marriage in the early Christian world, identifying

---

[2] For the details, see the list of Angelo Tosato's publications, *infra*.

its values]; and, finally, the essay "L'istituto famigliare dell'Antico Israele e della Chiesa primitiva", in *Anthropotes*, 1997. Alongside these works, among his many specific in-depth studies, we can recall:

(a) philological essays (on matrimonial language in the Old Testament, in *Annali dell'Istituto Orientale* di Napoli, 1983; on the meaning of the terms *'alma nût* ("widow"),*'almānût* ("widowhood"), in *Bibbia e Oriente*, 1983);

b) exegetical essays relating to passages particularly significant for matrimonial studies (on Mt 1, 19, Lev 18,18 and Gen 2,24 in 1979, 1984 and 1990 respectively, all in *Catholic Biblical Quarterly*, in English; on a previously unpublished fragment from the IV cave of Qumran, in *Biblica*, 1993);

(c) essays relating to specific institutional issues (on the marital consent of sons and daughters of the family, in *Studia et Documenta Historiae et Iuris*, 1985; on the transfer of goods occurring with the Israelitic marriage, in Bibbia e oriente, 1985][3].

(2) As for political institutions, it is worth mentioning: on Jesus and the Zealots, in *Bibbia e Oriente*, 1977; on theocracy in ancient Israel, in *Cristianesimo nella storia*, 1987; on the political conception of the Book of Chronicles, in *Ricerche storico-bibliche*, 1989; on the problem of political power for the Israelites at the time of Jesus, in *Estudios Biblicos*, 1990.

(3) Finally, as for economic institutions, it is worth mentioning the book *Economia di mercato e cristianesimo* (Quaderni del Centro di Metodologia delle Scienze Sociali, LUISS, Rome, Borla, 1994) [a collection of four essays, the first of which, "Cristianesimo e mercato", is a critical re-examination of the reading by Ludwig von Mises of gospel passages relating to economics, previously unpublished; the other three - "Cristianesimo e capitalismo (il problema esegetico di alcuni passi evangelici)", "Il vescovo è economista?" and "Magistero pontificio e Sacra Scrittura" - are revised versions of published works] and the essay "Il Vangelo e la ricchezza (per la fuoriuscita dai luoghi comuni)", published in the volume *Etica cattolica e società di mercato*, Venezia, Marsilio, 1997. On the subject of economics and Holy Scriptures, Tosato also has the merit of having promoted the publication in Italy of the book by Michael Novak, *Lo spirito del capitalismo*

---

[3] The majority of the writings of Angelo Tosato on the marital and family institutions of the Bible are collected in the volume ANGELO TOSATO, *Matrimonio e famiglia nell'Antico Israele e nella Chiesa primitiva*, Soveria Mannelli, Rubbettino, 2013.

democratico e il cristianesimo (Rome, Studium, 1987) and providing it with the biblical support it lacked[4].

The fundamental ambition of all these studies was one and the same: to grasp not only the "what", but also the "how" and the "why"; that is, through which historical process, in which circumstances, to answer to which needs and with which cultural conditionings did the biblical social models arise. The aim of the vast research hence seems to be: to provide the *prolegomena* necessary, on the one hand, for the elaboration of a faithful, enlightened and beneficial social teaching of the Church and, on the other, for reflection on the historic institutional forms of the Church itself.

Addendum, after 1997

Between 1995 and 1999, until the moment of his untimely death on 30 April, Angelo Tosato continued his teaching activity, expanding it to new courses (e.g., the course on matrimonial texts at the Pontifical Biblicum Institute). Similarly intense was his participation as a speaker in conferences and debates on political, economic and social themes, rich in implications for the social doctrine of the Church and scientific research, resulting in articles published *post mortem* (see nn. 51-57 in the list of publications). The study we propose here, translated in English, was completed only a few days before his death (see n. 57 in the bibliography). He considered it to be the work in which he brought together the reflections of his many years of biblical studies.

---

[4] The writings of Angelo Tosato on the relation between the Scriptures and wealth are collected in the volume ANGELO TOSATO, *Vangelo e Ricchezza. Nuove prospettive esegetiche*, Dario Antiseri, Francesco D'Agostino and Angelo Petroni (eds.), Soveria Mannelli, Rubbettino, 2002.

LIST OF ANGELO TOSATO'S PUBLICATIONS

1. *Per una revisione degli studi sulla* metanoia *neotestamentaria*, «Rivista Biblica Italiana» 23 (1975), pp. 3-45.
2. *Il battesimo di Gesù e alcuni passi trascurati dello Pseudo-Filone*, «Biblica» 56 (1975), pp. 405-409.
3. *La concezione giudaica del matrimonio al tempo di Gesù*, «Lateranum» n.s. 42 (1976), pp. 5-33.
4. *Il matrimonio nel giudaismo antico e nel Nuovo Testamento*, Città Nuova, Roma 1976.
5. *Il battesimo di Gesù e le Odi di Salomone*, «Bibbia e Oriente» 18 (1976), pp. 261-269.
6. *Gesù e gli zeloti alla luce delle Odi di Salomone*, «Bibbia e Oriente» 19 (1977), pp. 145-153.
7. *Ideologia rivoluzionaria e Gesù*, «Il Samaritano» n. 4 (1978), pp. 99-103.
8. *La colpa di Saul (1Sam 15,22-23)*, «Biblica» 59 (1978), pp. 251-259.
9. *The literary structure of the first two poems of Balaam (Num XXIII 7-10,18-24)*, «Vetus Testamentum» 29 (1978), pp. 98-106.
10. *Il ripudio: delitto e pena (Mal 2,10-16)*, «Biblica» 59 (1978), pp. 548-553.
11. *Magnum Patrimonium Commune (Nostra Aetate n. 4)*, «Lateranum» n.s. 45 (1979), pp. 36-59.
12. Intervento al Colloquio romanistico-canonistico, February 1978, Università Lateranense, *Atti del Colloquio romanistico-canonistico*, Febbraio 1978, «Utrumque Ius» (Collectio Pont. Univ. Later.) 4 (1979), pp. 449-450.
13. Recensione a Giuseppe Scarpat, *Il pensiero religioso di Seneca e l'ambiente ebraico e cristiano* (Paideia, Brescia 1977), «Rivista di Storia della Chiesa in Italia» 33 (1979), p. 243.
14. *Joseph, Being a Just Man (Matt 1:19)*, «Catholic Biblical Quarterly» 41 No. 4 (1979), pp. 547-551.
15. *Il matrimonio israelitico. Una teoria generale*, (Analecta Biblica, 100), Biblical Institute Press, Roma 1982 (and 2001).
16. *Sulle origini del termine* akrobystia *(prepuzio, incirconcisione)*, «Bibbia e Oriente» 24 (1982), pp. 43-49.

17. *Il sangue della circoncisione*, in *Sangue e Antropologia Biblica* (Atti della II Settimana di Studio), a cura di F. Vattioni, Ed. Pia Unione Preziosissimo Sangue, Roma 1982, vol. I, pp. 59-80.

18. *Il linguaggio matrimoniale veterotestamentario: stato degli studi* «Annali dell'Istituto Orientale di Napoli» 43 (1983), pp. 135-160.

19. *Processo generativo e sangue nell'antichità (saggio di ermeneutica biblica)*, in *Sangue e Antropologia Biblica* (Atti della III Settimana di Studio), a cura di F. Vattioni, Ed. Pia Unione Preziosissimo Sangue, Roma 1983, vol. II, pp. 643-696.

20. *I simboli dell'iniziazione: dall'Antico al Nuovo Testamento, I simboli dell'iniziazione cristiana* (Atti del I Congresso Internaz. di Liturgia) «Studia Anselmiana» 87 (Roma 1983), pp. 13-59.

21. *Sul significato dei termini 'almānâh, almānût*, «Bibbia e Oriente» 25 (1983), pp. 193-214.

22. *The Law of Lev 18:18. A Re-examination,* «Catholic Biblical Quarterly» 46 (1984), pp. 199-214.

23. *Il trasferimento dei beni nel matrimonio israelitico*, «Bibbia e Oriente» 145(1985), pp. 129-148.

24. *Sul consenso dei figli e delle figlie di famiglia nel matrimonio israelitico*, «Studia et Documenta Historiae et Iuris» 51 (1985), pp. 283-318.

25. *Il matrimonio israelitico (a proposito di una Nota)*, «Studia et Documenta Historiae et Iuris» 51 (1985), pp. 393-401.

26. Recensione a Pietro Dacquino, *Storia del matrimonio cristiano alla luce della Bibbia* (LDC, Leumann 1984), «Biblica» 66 (1985), pp. 444-446.

27. Recensione a *Le canon de l'Ancien Testament. Sa formation et son histoire* (a cura di J.-D., Kaestlie e O. Wermelinger, Labor et Fides, Genève 1984) «Cristianesimo nella storia» 7 (1986), pp. 177-179.

28. *L'onore di una donna in Israele* [osservazioni a proposito di C. Locher, *Die Ehre einer Frau in Israel* (Orbis Biblicus et Orientalis, 70), Universitätsverlag Vandenhoeck & Ruprecht, Freiburg Schweiz-Göttingen 1986], «Biblica» 68 (1987), pp. 268-276.

29. La teocrazia nell'antico Israele. Genesi e significato di una forma costituzionale, «Cristianesimo nella Storia» 8 (1987), pp. 1-50.

30. Presentazione di M. Novak, *Lo spirito del capitalismo democratico e il cristianesimo* (Studium, Roma 1987, pp. IX-XXXV).

31. *Cristianesimo e capitalismo. Il problema esegetico di alcuni passi evangelici*, «Rivista Biblica» 35 (1987), pp. 465-476.

32. *Lettera al Direttore di Segno Sette*, «Segno Sette», anno 6, nn. 28-29, 12-19 luglio 1988, p. 25.

33. Presentazione di *Pietro nel Nuovo Testamento* (R.E. Brown, K.P. Donfried e J. Reumann eds.), Borla, Roma,1988, pp. 5-11.

34. *Israele nell'ideologia politica del Cronista*, (Atti del V Convegno di studi veterotestamentari), «Ricerche Storico Bibliche» I/1 (1989), pp. 257-269.

35. Recensione a J. Jeremias, *Das Königtum Gottes in den Psalmen. Israels Begegnung mit der kanaanäischen Mythos in der Jahwe-König-Psalmen* (Forschungen zur Religion und Literatur des Alten und Neuen Testaments, 141, Vandenhoeck & Ruprecht, Göttingen 1987), «Cristianesimo nella Storia» 10 (1989), pp. 615-616.

36. *On Gen 2:24*, «Catholic Biblical Quarterly» 52 (1990), pp. 389-409.

37. Il problema del potere politico per gli Israeliti del tempo di Gesù, «Estudios Biblicos» 48 (1990), pp. 461-487.

38. *Le mariage dans l'Ancien Testament*, «Masses Ouvrières», fasc. 439, sept.-oct. (1991), pp. 25-34.

39. *Magistero pontificio e Sacra Scrittura (due pagine di storia)*, «Anthropotes» 8 (1992), pp. 239-272.

40. *Su di una norma matrimoniale 4QD*, «Biblica» 74 (1993), pp. 401-410.

41. *Il vescovo è economista?* Intervista rilasciata a Tullio Meli, «Giornale di Sicilia», 7 febbraio (1994), p. 53.

42. *Economia di mercato e* cristianesimo, Quaderni del Centro di Metodologia delle Scienze Sociali, LUISS, 11, Borla, Roma, 1994.

43. Intervista rilasciata a Pierangela Rossi per «Avvenire», 27-30 gennaio (1995) (uscita deformata).

44. Ristampa di due saggi di Economia di mercato e cristianesimo, D. Antiseri, Cattolici a difesa del mercato, SEI, Torino 1995, pp. 333-364.

45. Review to G. Barbiero, L'asino del nemico. Rinuncia alla vendetta e amore del nemico nella legislazione dell'Antico Testamento (Es 23,4-5; Dt 22,1-4; Lv 19,17-18) (Analecta Biblica, 128, Pontificio Istituto Biblico, Roma 1991), «Cristianesimo nella Storia» 17 (1995), pp. 173-176.

46. *Solidarietà e profitto: il ruolo degli imprenditori*, «Biblioteca della libertà» (Centro Luigi Einaudi) 133 (1996), pp. 45-56

47. *Dall'economismo ad una economia per l'uomo, Le sfide del secolarismo e l'avvenire della fede*, Urbaniana University Press, Roma 1996,

pp. 153-185 (Relazione tenuta il 1° dicembre 1995 al Colloquio Internazionale promosso dalla Pontificia Università Urbaniana di Roma e dal Pontificio Consiglio per la Cultura su "Alle soglie del III Millennio. Le sfide del secolarismo e l'avvenire della fede" (Roma, 30 nov.-2 dic. 1995).

48. *Gesù e il benessere delle nazioni*, Mercato e finanza per lo sviluppo e l'occupazione: i comportamenti etici nella nuova Europa, Atti della 4[a] Conferenza "Etica ed Economia", Foligno 10 nov. 1995, Nemetria 4, Assisi 1996, pp. 56-60.

49. *Il vangelo e la ricchezza (per la fuoriuscita dai luoghi comuni), in* D. Antiseri, M. Novak, A. Tosato, M. Zoller, *Etica cattolica e società di mercato*, a cura di A.M. Petroni, Marsilio, Venezia 1997, pp. 89-197 (Conferenza di Torino, Unione Industriale di Torino, 21 febbraio 1996; Conferenza di Biella, UCID, 22 febbraio 1996).

50. *L'istituto famigliare dell'antico Israele e della Chiesa primitiva*, «Anthropotes» 13 (1997), pp. 109-174.

51. *I reati matrimoniali denunciati in 4QMMT, Biblica et Semitica*. Studi in memoria di Francesco Vattioni, a cura di L. Cagni; Istituto Universitario Orientale, Dipartimento di Studi Asiatici, Series Minor, LIX, Napoli 1999, pp. 645-666.

52. *I primi richiami di Paolo in tema matrimoniale (1 Ts 4, 3-8), in Studi sul Vicino Oriente antico dedicati alla memoria di Luigi Cagni*, a cura di S. Graziani, Istituto Universitario Orientale, Dipartimento di Studi Asiatici, Series Minor, LXI, Napoli 2000, pp. 2193-2218.

53. *Lc 20, 34-36: il matrimonio non si addice a cristiani e cristiane*, in *Donum natalicium*. Studi in onore di Claudio Saporetti in occasione del suo 60° compleanno, a cura di P. Negri Scafa e P. Gentili, Borgia, Roma 2000, pp. 255-294.

54. *Vangelo e* Libertà, in *Cattolicesimo e Liberalismo*, Atti del Convegno di Studi, Certosa di Pontignano-Università degli Studi di Siena, 16-17 ottobre 1998, a cura di A. Cardini e F. Pulitini, Rubbettino, Soveria Mannelli 2000, pp. 85-148.

55. Recensione a F. Rossier, *L'intercession entre les hommes dans la Bible hébraïque. L'in- tercession entre les hommes aux origines de l'intercession auprès de Dieu* (Orbis Biblicus et Orientalis, 152), Universitätsverlag-Vandenhoeck & Ruprecht, Freiburg Schweiz-Göttingen 1996, «Cristianesimo nella Storia» 20 (1999) 191-192.

56. Recensione a G. Ricciotti, *Storia di Israele* (ristampa con Presenta-

zione di P. Sacchi e Introduzione di A. Erba, SEI, Torino 1997), «Cristianesimo nella Storia» 20 (1999), pp. 699-701.

57. *Lo statuto cattolico dell'interpretazione della Bibbia*, «Ars Interpretandi. Annuario di ermeneutica giuridica» 4 (1999), pp. 123-200.

Finito di stampare
nel mese di aprile 2021
dalla
Scuola Tipografica S. Pio X
Via degli Etruschi, 7
00185 Roma